Lilith
Queen of Demons

Gillian Macdonald

BLACK MOON PUBLISHING
CINCINNATI, OHIO USA

Black Moon Manifesto

It is the Will and mission of Bate Cabal/Black Moon to effectively manifest unique and insightful occult Works for the esoteric community in a manner that is unfettered by commercial considerations.

BlackMoonPublishing.com

Design and layout by
Jo Bounds of Black Moon

ISBN: 978-1-890399-70-2

United States • United Kingdom • Canada • Europe • Australia • India

Acknowledgements

Thanks to Pier Ruaro for his help in researching some of the content of this book. To Cain Helsson for his friendship and encouragement. To Pete Gotto of Green Magic Publishing for publishing my early books. Especially to Diane Narraway for supporting my artistic endeavours and introducing me to Black Moon. To those who tried to dissuade me from writing it and those who encouraged me, you know who you are. To Mishlen Linden, Nic Messner and Rupert Desnaux for the inspiring art they contributed. And to all those at Black Moon Publishing for believing it to be worthy of sharing with the esoteric and occult community.

Lilith Child by Gillian Macdonald

CONTENTS

Editors' Foreword

This book provides the reader with the tools necessary to come to a greater understanding of the historical, political, and spiritual significance of Lilith, as she has been perceived, and expressed throughout history.

How is it that a deity with roots that go back deep into the furthest recesses of ancestor memory, and one that represents everything that is wild, untamable, violent dark and destructive still finds relevance with today's culture? Her very name can still evoke terror in a pregnant woman of the 21st century, and her existence is quoted as proof of the female life force to subvert, and destroy patriarchal expectations of female subordination. It is unclear as to how she was ever worshipped except as a malignant force to be warded off, and yet she was around at the very beginning of humanity's efforts to explain the invisible world.

Reflections of her archetype can be seen in Queen Sheba, the whore of Babalon. She is quoted in Hebrew texts as being created as Adams equal, what could possibly go wrong?

Religious institutions have based major parts of their apocrypha and outer teachings on the denouncement and excoriation of the role of the wild, untamed woman, precisely because she is the largest threat to everything they represent. Lilith remains relevant now as she has throughout human history, she is capable of destroying any status quo, as are her followers!

– Maegdlyn Morris
Associate Editor

There is a radical aliveness before a great storm that infuses being. The attention becomes anchored in an unfathomable moment. Lilith is written on the face of the sky. The heavens are tearing. Sounding a deep lament before dropping their tears into the streets and gutters fertile with past and the morrow's hopes and fears all soon to be washed away. There is no refuge from this Storm. When the levee breaks there's no place to hide. She rides within the heart of the storm. Wake Up...She is in the air. Wake Up...She howls as the wind in a language that unravels the predictable.

As Gill Macdonald writes, we develop a relationship with our personal Lilith. This points to mine. Lilith embraces me most often as the Storm, both physically and in allegory. Mademoiselle Katrina descended upon New Orleans and my world was changed. So much gone so quickly. Only the Mysteries remained inviolate, unfathomable. A Tibetan lama advised me, "You lost everything. Hold onto that feeling." Words worthy of Lilith. A teaching worthy of the Mysteries.

There is a certain soft comfort in believing that life is predictable. In truth, how many events in our lives are predictable? Lilith breathes life into the moment and life is not soft and comfortable. Strength trumps complacency.

Lilith has not fared well in historical accounts, but then who writes such "accounts"? Men, over and over again the words of men. Nary a woman's voice to be found in this past. Black Moon is proud to present Lilith in a woman's voice.

– Dr. Louie Martinié
Editor

Lilith by Mishlen Linden

INTRODUCTION

This book introduces people to the practice of working spiritually with Lilith. It provides insight into her extensive background and offers guidance on how to identify with your Lilith. It is not and cannot be a fully comprehensive book on Lilith, my path is a living one, constantly expanding in knowledge and experience. For readers who have little or no experience of Lilith I hope that this book provides a basic introduction and guide to gaining some understanding and deepening their own connection with her. For the more advanced, this text can provide both reference material and hopefully new light on an ancient deity. A basic working structure and several tried and tested rites to the Lilith's within the scope of my experience are provided.

It seems to me that unless you are actively working with Lilith and understand at least a little of her nature she has this almost taboo reputation. Lilith seems to come with a health warning.

True she can, and has, sent many over the edge of sanity into places of the psyche and soul that few wish to travel but Lilith is not alone in receiving such a reaction. I feel that facing this projected fear and overcoming it is part of the Lilith journey. Once the fear is dropped, with humility not arrogance, then if she wishes it to be, it can be conquered. But a massive part in her role as Queen of the Night or Dark Moon is to encourage us to explore and embrace our own shadow selves. To not shy away from all the murky, hidden, suppressed aspects of our personalities or those of humanities as a whole. She helps us strip away any conditioning that led to us denying these parts of self that we know society frowns upon or are seen as less than celestial. She brings all our destructive, darker, devilish thoughts to the surface and says "Deal with them, accept

them, they are a part of you, a part of humanity". This is where many have issue with Lilith and other of her kin. Sure, there might be serious self destructive urges, or desires to harm others but it is my belief and experience that it is more a case of finding a dynamically balanced outlet for these impulses.

So unless you are currently seriously psychologically unbalanced allowing your shadow out into the light for you to see shouldn't really lead to dreadful consequence. If your shadow is where you hide your true shame, or guilt or secret desires then facing up to them and exploring them within safe and legal parameters is part of working with Lilith. This especially applies to sexual ones. They are a large part of her nature. Here Lilith will aid you in coming to terms with them and link you with others sharing the same desires. This also makes her unpopular. But it really is a case of each to their own and sexual liberation might well be her thing but there are many other layers to Lilith. Her boundaries are non-existent and ours are more evident. So it becomes less about Lilith and also more so at the same time. As she brings you closer to your own desires she reveals hers.

Religious establishments have spent thousands of years tarring those who walk the shadows with being threats to society, where as in truth we rarely ever are. Liberating ourselves from these constraints and allowing free expression is not always comfortable for those around us. In a simplified nutshell, Lilith reacts and responds to what inspires and motivates you the most especially if it relates to your shadow being the most alive through it. She then works with this to create new windows of expression for whatever this energy happens to be.

But to attempt, like many on a New Age spiritual path, to rise above base urges is to deny them and in so doing you deny an aspect of divinity. It causes separation rather than a more wholesome integration. This is where Lilith is, she is fully integrated, her

darkness casts shadows in the light but the contrast is required, for that is life, life is full of contrasting energies. And this doesn't mean that she isn't going to aid you in any changes you wish to make, far from it, if it is your desire deep down to change then she often gives the strength and guides you towards that aspiration. The easier these windows of opportunity are to see through the more one wants it without any fear attached. But the more resistance then the more she pushes. As a wise man once said to me, "It is as if Lilith always needs something to push against, a resistance" and I thought yes, she likes to flex warrior muscles occasionally. Ultimately she isn't known for pushing to breaking point but some might disagree. She takes you to where you know you need to go.

Lilith's children come from all walks of life and a myriad of spiritual paths or traditions, many being solitary practitioners of magical arts. That having been said there are numerous covens dedicated to her and all have their own unique relationship and take on her. If I have learned anything from her it is that she cannot, and will not, be boxed in or definitively identified and tamed in any way. Making any claims to being connected to an ultimate Lilith is often found to be a false folly. Those who know her best are still surprised by her twists and turns and seemingly endless revelations. To me this is a large part of the attraction, you are never bored with Lilith in your life.

We can trace her earliest recorded names back to ancient Mesopotamia and perhaps ever further too ancient Anatolia but it is the Jewish Lilith who is best known. I wanted to get to the roots of this Lilith, to the meat on her bones, and to the depth of her soul, to the Lilith I have become used to and feel I know well yet often struggle trying to describe to people.

Others have done this before, there are other books on Lilith, more academic ones, as well as a plethora of non-academic fiction and non-fiction but I hope this book will be different. Here I have

explored all I have been able to discover of her origins and the many Liliths that grew into the eventual modern day one. As well as this, I give you a basic working structure onto which you can build your own spiritual relationship with her.

Her role in the Apocrypha is well known and this this Lilith of the apocalypse, who may or may not have been in part inspiration for the Whore of Babalon, is a literal abomination to any who oppose freedom and liberation. And as such she is often linked in with the feminist movement. Freedom of choice is a major part of her modern evolution. And that goes for men as well as women. So although she is held up as a feminist icon this is not necessarily, nor has ever really been, her sole role. I'd see her as way more than this. She has her place in the hidden side of the Tree of Life or Qliphoth, and is an integral part of diabolical and infernal gnostic paths.

When making a study of her, it often appears as if as if myths accredited to versions of Lilith seem to arrive when great shifts in human consciousness occur. These have inevitably lead onto major change and revolutions and as such they are rarely comfortable. Some of her early roots are almost definitely in the realms of storm demons making her currents or streams of a sudden and sometimes unpleasant revolutionary nature.

She was there at the birth of religion in the Middle East and in turn evolved alongside the birth of agriculture and larger organised structured societies and cities. She had a side role to play in the discovery of metallurgy and all that has led on from it arriving in our lives. Like a giant spider in an eternal web she has a finger on all pulses of human evolution. As each thread is cast so she weaves another link. And if any land on her web she knows in an instant.

She is the hyper-sensitive and ultra-aware mother of all, nothing gets past her. As each civilisation rose and fell and cultures gained dominance and lost, so Lilith re-created herself. Until she reached Judaism. Here as Biblical texts tell us, she finds her repose. And in

many respects the Lilith we have today is mostly the Jewish one.

But it is also possible she had a name change and is ushering in the apocalyptic times astride the beast. It is impossible to avoid such world-views when dealing with Lilith. As to what variety of revelation this apocalypse might produce, who knows. Some say it is a constant on going apocalypse and that veils are constantly being lifted as one travels one's spiritual path and that as such each person's apocalypse is unique to them and their own journey's. Though born of primal times she is very much part of the energies in this time and our level of existence.

She appeared as first born and the one who moves Yahweh into creating humankind and the world in some Jewish scriptures beginning life. Simplified this would break down into her energy being the creatrix force and his the masculine needed for future re-birth. As she becomes his consort this could be viewed as her re-elevation to celestial heavens but that is only one perspective and, many would argue, only one Lilith.

But it is the evil or more destructive side to her nature that she is not only most well-known for but also seems to invoke the most fear. Her baby killing, life force stealing, soul possessing vampire nature invokes terror, to this day. I'm not about to defend her here. She can be all of the above. Her reputation as a 'terrible mother' exists to this day. And as nature is a cruel mistress so is Lilith, often the cruellest of all.

We only have to open our eyes fully to see all manner of pain and suffering in life and accept that, whether we like it or not, this is nature. Wishing to rise above this and strive for a world free of such things seems a part of the more modern day human condition. But Lilith forces our eyes back on the very real and true nature of nature. All life is born of death and the route back to this can often be fraught with pain and suffering along the way. She was born of the same death as we all are. Accepting this and not attempting to

avoid it or side step it in any way is part of her path.

This is partly why she is not embraced by many on the many so called 'New Age' paths. Those with rigid ethics, morals and laws have no place in Lilith's world any more than those attempting to rise up and ascend to a celestial heaven. She does not recognise such things. Lilith is freedom full of potential and chaos from which anything you wish can be moulded regardless of human rules. So to many it seems that Lilith anchors us down in the very Earth of existence.

Magically she reveals the paths and systems that work. Those that have been around for thousands of years. The lady herself seems able to adapt to most of them for to Lilith good and evil are always subjective. She can be beauty and grace, laughter and joy, sexual predator, seductress, tempter, reveller, among a hundred other things besides but she also anchors us down in the darkness, the underworld amid the dead and the grime and filth and disease of humanity. From here we can only seek to rise up. To find ourselves back on earth and now able to reach out above and reach out all around us, to see her underworld portal as a link to magical dimensions that we can then learn to tap into and utilise.

From a philosophical view point it is possible to say that all she does is hold up her dark mirror to your most hidden aspects and draw out your fears and your own most destructive and evil parts forcing you to face them. And as a child of Lilith I would agree that she does this to most at some point of their journey. But I am not alone in feeling that there is a tendency these days to over philosophise upon spiritual beings and our relationships with them. It does help to have a basic understanding of magical processes and some sort if training in esoteric arts before opening up to Lilith but your relationship with her will be yours, unique, and ever evolving. Lilith can weave many a veil and twist one's mind into endless knots so it often pays to go with the more experiential connection and

intuitively feel ones way than rely heavily on analysis or philosophy.

Everyone who has any sort of relationship with Lilith has their own very strong feelings about her. To me each of them is probably as valid as another. As the lady herself prefers to remain partly mysterious then it will always be impossible for any of us to say we truly know her in all her glory. Some see her as purely a nocturnal Queen of Vampires using our psychic energy to connect with others and feed from the unsuspecting and willing donors. But to me this is only one facet of the greater Lilith.

I often wonder if Dion Fortune was a Lilith child and if Moon Magic was her contribution to the Lilith story. Her main character has Lilith traits and uses psychic energy to tap into a man she is stalking/in love with. Some see Lilith as the ultimate Femme Fatale, the one men cannot resist and yet wish they had! Some interpret her as a Creatrix, the first born human now immortalised in her pre-Eve role. For what we have to remember about her is that she is akin to legion, she is one but many. So we all meet a different Lilith, or many.

Many are inspired by her in a creative manner. But this is not the same as invoking her and working closely in a spiritual sense or being chosen for partial or full possession by her. The latter requires working at a magical and ritualistic level.

This book aims to aid you in your own personal journey with her. It includes invocations, rites and general advice. These are not strongly based on traditional grimoires. Nor are they heavily drawn from either the Right Hand Path or Left Hand Path Kabbala/Qabbala. I have given some brief inclusion of some of these paths but as they are not ones I am initiated into I cannot write with authority on them. So I have had to travel my own path. Over the first few years of working with Lilith it seemed as though she steered me away from reading anyone else's work on her.

She wanted me to have an unbiased purely experiential

relationship with her. This was not an easy road to tread. And not one I would advise. Living mythology is rarely a wise move.

I'd have been far better informed and less likely to discover them the hard way if I'd just read about them instead. Still it gave me what has been described as a 'two headed connection' at times. Having Lilith take up residence in ones psyche is not the same as a possession though if it happens to you there will be many who, often through fear, will cast that accusation. She becomes a wise muse. A greater intelligence. But can only work with what is already there and in my case I sometimes feel for her.

Her ability to inspire creatively can become akin to an intoxicating euphoric drug often bordering on the manic. And this alone can lead others to see Lilith inspired folk as having occasional mental health issues. When you mix this with her more sombre and gloomy twilight energy it can become easy to mistake it for deeper problems. As it is she is all extremes and all in between and can be anything energy wise you wish to draw upon. The highs and lows of the naturally creative are mimicked but to slightly exaggerated levels. This doesn't rule out the possibility of Lilith's children having such issues. We are as vulnerable as any. But it is possible, with her help, to tap into her varied currents and work them to our own ends without major problems or incarcerations!

Each person's approach to this working relationship with differ. Some might prefer to keep it at the romanticised inspirational level. Others seek Lilith through both simple or complex rituals and strict traditional methods. And some prefer a more intuitive approach. But one thing that does seem to occur no matter how deeply one travels into her realms, she calls you and often it is due to being close to another of her kin. This selective perspective is not always viewed clearly. Many I know of have tried to connect with her and not even skimmed the surface.

Being a child of Lilith doesn't make you special or elitist, there

is no hierarchy here, simply your allegiance. In the same way you are born into a particular family on this plane so you also have a spiritual family. Lilith knows her children and she will make herself known, whether you chose to answer her calling is entirely up to you. Merely having been drawn to her is a calling in itself, as is usually the way with many spiritual entities. I haven't as yet met anyone she has refused to work with but have found that some have had to try differing doors, so to speak, before finding their Lilith and the route she wants them to take with her.

Modern life is so artificial. Lilith energy can at times feel raw and primal, it can often feel as if she has more affinity with tribes still living in primitive ways than contemporary folk. Yet in our modern scientific and technological age or plastic fantastic polluted hell, whichever way you view it, she has found her repose.

Quoting from Isaiah 34:

12: Her nobles shall be no more, nor shall kings be proclaimed there; all her princes are gone. 13: Her castles shall be overgrown with thorns, her fortresses with thistles and briers. She shall become an abode for jackals and a haunt for ostriches. 14: Wildcats shall meet with desert beasts, satyrs shall call to one another; There shall the Lilith repose, and find for herself a place to rest. 15: There the hoot owl shall nest and lay eggs, hatch them out and gather them in her shadow; There shall the kites assemble, none shall be missing its mate. 16: Look in the book of the LORD and read: No one of these shall be lacking, For the mouth of the LORD has ordered it, and His spirit shall gather them there. 17: It is He who casts the lot for them, and with His hands He marks off their shares of her; They shall possess her forever, and dwell there from generation to generation.

And she them.

Lilith–Queen of Demons by Gillian Macdonald

Chapter One

Queen of Demons
Ancient Mesopotamia

The name Lilith seems to have stemmed from several possible roots in Ancient Mesopotamia. And over a gradual evolution of several thousand years she eventually becomes the Jewish Lilith that most people are familiar with. Her earliest beginnings might well have been born of oral traditions predating recorded history in the region. This would, however, be difficult to prove so it is to the ancient mythologies and archaeological evidence that most turn to when researching Lilith's origins.

Some call her "The Queen of Demons" and view her as such, and there is no denying some of her demonic roots. One of the earliest contenders for the eventual role of Lilith is found in ancient Assyria and Sumer. Here you can find tell of a demon, or collection of them, known as Lil·itu. Not much is written on Lil·itu who is mainly mentioned as a Sumerian and Assyrian storm demon or collection of said spirits. As to the word 'demon' in this case it pertains to any spirits who cause both wanted and unwanted effects. The emphasis is on them being able to do harm or good but also for this two sided coin to operate simultaneously as is so often reflected in life. Demons were thought by both the Assyrians and Sumerians to be controlled by the will of the Gods. And, one supposes, created by them. We tend to view all demons in the negative as purely evil beings hell bent on causing harm but they can be allies as well.

Jewish texts have titles for all manner of demons and most tend to be male so this is another reason that Lilith stands out. The most popular name is *shedim* which stems from the Assyrian *shedu*.

According to Raphael Patai in his book *The Hebrew Goddess* there are at least four recorded Sumerian and Assyrian demons; all considered interconnected, with Lil-litu. The first and second ones are known as Lilu/ masculine and Lili / feminine. As he doesn't go into great detail about them I decided to try with my limited resources to find out a little bit more. The word for demon in Assyrian and Akkadian is sometimes known as Alu, though it can also relate to a particular demon of this name. A famous Alu is the father of Gilgamesh and is recorded as being, Lilu. This is an excerpt from the Sumerian King List describing some demonic attributes.

The wicked Utukku (demon) who slays man alive on the plain.
The wicked Alu who covers (man) like a garment. (possesses)
The wicked Etimmu, the wicked Gallu, (Underworld demons/devils)
*   who bind the body.*
The Lamme (Goddess/Demon Lamashtu), the Lammea and Labasu
*   (Believed to be demons employed by Lamashtu - see later context*
*   Vampires), who cause disease in the body.*
The Lilu who wanders in the plain.
They have come nigh unto a suffering man on the outside.
They have brought about a painful malady in his body.

So here we have an early account of a masculine demon employed by Lamashtu to cause illness to men who are out on 'the plain'. The plain might refer to the Plain of Shinar or land of Babylon but is also a term used to describe Edin/Eden (This at a much later date being adopted by the Jewish scriptures). That the demon/s afflict the outside of the person first then permeating inwards would indicate a skin disease or burn that becomes infected, either way it

has a demonic cause. The female Lili and possible Lilith connection seems to home in more on women and infants. These beings are most definitely seen as demons and not deities. The Lili tends to get associated with the desert or wilderness but plain is a similar translation and is often associated with land that needed irrigation so near a river but not green, more desert. This is not quite the true wilderness people link Lilith in with. But for those familiar with her liminal nature to find her in a place between places makes perfect sense. Lili was a demon who attacked pregnant women and infants and here we have the earliest link with one of the many evil attributes of the Jewish Lilith. Next in the four we have Ardat-lili also known as Vardat-lili this is a succubus. Her very name means 'maiden lilu' or maiden demon. She is a frustrated bride but never marries. She is incapable of normal sex and cannot bare children. She takes her frustrations out aggressively on young men in a sexual manner whilst they sleep. And yet again we have qualities most who are familiar with Lilith will recognise. But Lilitu is also accredited with being part of a triad, it hasn't been agreed upon among scholars but some propose that the Akkadian Lilitu, Lilu and Ardat-lili are one. Lili and Ardat-lili being seen as the same being in some cases. With Lilitu also being seen as a sacred prostitute, Lilu her consort and Aradat-lili the barren maid they produce. This is not the usual trinity of mother, father and holy son. More an unholy trinity of demons.

But Lil-litu is alleged to be an androgynous evil storm demon that come in from wild places to prey upon children and women taking them up with her/him into the air. It is night and dark, pitch black, an unholy sound can be heard far off in the distance. And as people lay in their beds trying to sleep all they can hear is this howling coming closer and closer. A storm is arriving. With it comes uncertainty, how much damage will it cause, will they survive it? Are they to be kept awake by it all night listening to the hell it is

Lilitu by Gillian Macdonald

raining down upon them? And hearing the animals scream as their less substantial shelters are ripped and torn apart leaving them exposed to the cruel and harsh skin searing sand. Or worse having their own roof ripped up and house exposed as lives are literally threatened by this beast. And as if this isn't enough you are lying there terrified it is an actual demon who might literally take you up into the air and cause you to disappear into a void never to be seen again. Whether there is a literal connection between the

appearance of a storm and Lili/Lilu or Lilitu's arrival is debatable. Some tornadoes are capable of lifting people into the air but it is more likely an analogy between the two than literal. The sudden unexpected chaos this demon causes is akin to the same damage a storm can cause. That having been said sandstorms come from the desert regions and wilder places so the two have commonalities. Storm demons and Gods etc. are common to many ancient cultures. But as with all myths we have a chicken and egg scenario. Does a demon cause a storm and deliberately stir it up? Or is it a human need to explain a storm that gives birth to that demon? My view aligns with the ancient peoples and is that this is more spiritual and less philosophical. The demon causes the storm. The storms arrival marks the arrival of said demon. Having storms that are strong enough to carry women and children up into the air is not out of the question, rare, but possible. So it is to extreme storms perhaps we need to look.

Another way of understanding storm demons is to see them as 'spiritual' whirlwinds and not literal storms at all. But vortex's, sources of inspiration/air, dramatic realisations, sudden awakenings, dramatic revelations that occur on inner planes. The storm demon then arrives and has an effect similar to The Tower in Tarot, it breaks down preexisting out dated and no longer required forms allowing for new ones to be built.

The original seven evil *shebu* of Mesopotamia arrived as storm demons but became winged bulls with protective powers. Their power to previously destroy is honed and conjured, harnessed and used to inflict harm upon others who pose as a threat. This controlling and influencing by 'magical means' becoming more popular as time goes on. But didn't apply directly to Lilitu or her family. The storm initiates change, forced change, it costs in time money and resources, it depletes those and is feared for its ability to harm or kill. Any who have experienced a hurricane or caught in

the path of a tornado know only too well how terrifying it is. This is nature in one of her most dramatic forms.

The starry night reveals the heavens and allows people to glimpse beyond the clouds and blue of the day time. The ancient mindset was different to ours. Their world views were significantly affected by mysteries. Their limited sciences hadn't offered an explanation for many of the things we now take for granted. And so the radical difference between the intense warmth and colour of the sky in the area by day compared to the night was only understood through mythos. Here lie the birth of the Mesopotamian creation mysteries. Here resides the sky God Anu. And it is the night storms in particular that relate to Lilitu and later Lilith. She is the dark, dangerous side to the nocturnal heavens. For although the beneficent deities reside there aligned with their heavenly celestial bodies so do the demons. The stars themselves often accredited with being deities and demons. As one observes the movement of the stars so it is noticed that they are not fixed, they move and only one appears a constant that of the North Star. The blinking of Algol is visible to the naked eye and can at certain times be seen doing so. If in the case of Mesopotamia the worst storms come in winter when Algol is visible then it is Lilitu and later Lilith arriving. It is also pertinent to mention here that in many cultures including theirs, Witches are thought to ride storms.

The androgynous nature of this demon or demons is also interesting as many who work with Lilith today connect with her duality. And it seems a concept that lasts well into the future psyches of the Jewish Lilith that follows. The Akkadian Ardat-lili is also seen as a storm demon and is sometimes described as a mythical bird that is capable of carrying off women and children. Of all Middle Eastern birds only the Eagle is big enough to fly above storms and land safely after one. The Anzu bird is the one Akkadian speaking peoples associate with Ardat-lili and is a servant of the God Enlil

who at one time stole the 'tablets of destiny'.

Here we have an Akkadian text that says this of her;

"He, on whom Ardat-lili has cast her eyes,
The man, whom Ardat-lili has thrown to the ground..
Ardatu, on whom the man throws himself differently from on a
*   woman.*
Ardatu who has not opened her dress to a man,
Ardatu who does not dress before her husband"

This seems to be a form of warning to men to be watchful for these apparently virginal spirits who would have them and take them as they would a woman. The Ardat-lili is the force that throws the man into submission and the Ardatu the succubus who then has her way with him.

The Ardat-lili has her roots in Sumer and was incorporated into Akkadian and later Babylonian minds and beliefs. She is nocturnal, she comes to them whilst they sleep and she is strongly sexual. From a less spiritual perspective the higher incidence of men being visited by a succubus would lead some to think that it was merely a way of apportioning blame for wet dreams. The Lilith of Hebrew texts that most people are familiar with has these qualities. But to some extent this one also incorporates the incubus who visits women. For anyone who has had one visit there is a vast difference between these entities visiting you and wet dreams. So I would argue that it is more common for people to have strongly sexual dreams than be visited by a succubus or incubus. One persists beyond dream time into waking reality giving the sense of a physical presence, the other dissipates as you wake. And it is not so strange to see how Lilitu the nocturnal storm demon might have become Ardat-lili.

It is often thought that taking a man's seed enables her to create her demons. This association is common to most succubus myths. For

why else take the seed if it is not needed or required? It is possible that a spirit like Ardat-lili only wanted to feed the sexual energy of the men she visited? She had to need more from them and she must be making more demons with the seed. And common to the Lilitu myth is the presence of Ardat-lilu her male counterpart who would visit women and impregnate them with demonic children. And so the incubus is born. Ardat-lili is also cited as Liliths aid or maid. This direct link or relationship is another sign that she is evolving into what will eventually become the Lilith we are all more familiar with. The Ardat-lili cannot have sex in a normal way or bare children. This demonic force is out to threaten that which it can never aspire to being.

And another theory is that these demons steal seed to create hybrids/magical people who are half man half demon/spiritual entity, the mythical being Merlin being once such account.

Thus far we have beings that are both found in Assyrian and Sumerian mythologies and folklore. They are associated with the element of air. They prey on pregnant women and infants and also play the role of a succubus. They are destructive, terrifying, can take on male and female roles and are associated with storms, the deserts and wildernesses.

But the dichotomy of relating a storm demon to a succubus is confusing at best. The two seem worlds apart. And I can only surmise that this is due to them being two distinctly different entities with similar sounding names or that perhaps, as often happens, something was lost in the translation.

When exploring the oldest roots of Lilith it is inevitable that you find yourself examining ancient Mesopotamia. For those who only relate to the Jewish Lilith then this might not be a consideration or concern. But to those of us who sense her more ancient manifestations then it is impossible not to be curious about them. The area we think of as Ancient Mesopotamia was, as we

know, the birthplace of modern Western civilization. The Middle East is a melting pot of cultures, beliefs and religions, it always has been ever since people began settling there and probably always will be. Here complex languages evolved and the first cities were built. By the time of Lilitu, Ardat-lili and other demons like these the establishment of agriculture, metallurgy and religion had already arrived via migrating peoples from the north west in Anatolia and north east from the Russian Steppes. People from both of these areas had developed new skills such as agriculture, metallurgy and horsemanship and very early sciences such as mathematics and astronomy. The development of cuneiform writing enabled them to keep administration records and develop these sciences including medicine. They were also well versed in engineering, military and creating laws etc. the list goes on but it all adds up to the basic fundamental underlying infrastructure required for most civilizations and cities to exist.

The Assyrian culture is thought to have been in existence around 2,400 - 605 BCE. They shared a religion with the Sumerians further south, their pantheon of Gods and Goddesses being almost identical. Akkadian eventually replaced Sumerian as the dominant language of the area and remained so for some time. They were empire builders and very much a warrior race of peoples. Having evolved from the harsh mountainous and desert landscape they were, and still are very tough people and I see them as resilient survivors. The oldest settlements in this area stem back to 7,100 BCE and were Neolithic with the earliest signs of agriculture and pottery beginning to emerge but it is the discovery of metallurgy that caused the second biggest cultural shift after agriculture in the Anatolian and Mesopotamian area. So we are not dealing with primitive people here. The pre-cursors to the Jewish Lilith came from here and although a vast geographical area separated ancient Mesopotamia from the land that the Hebrews settled in the two

had common origins. People have always migrated and traveled for numerous reasons. The myths that end up in the scriptures of the Jewish peoples mostly came from further East from places such as Persia, India and even China. And as people such as Abraham took his people west so the mythology of his roots traveled with him.

To find Lilith evident at this time is pertinent to her mystery. She always seems to rise up to the surface or penetrate our plane of existence whenever mankind makes another massive change in lifestyle. She is there when all forms of revolution strike. Be they religious, agricultural, industrial, technological, sexual etc. She is there. And she is a lady of many faces and guises.

Another proposed contender in the mystery is Ninlil. Taking the element of air as a spiritual and elemental sign of her presence and then looking to see what spiritual beliefs and deities there are associated with it in Assyria and Sumer we find one Goddess who stands out more than others. And once we look at her story it is possible to see some parallels with later ones to emerge. This lady is Ninlil. For those unfamiliar with her story here is a condensed version. The Sumerians called her "Lady of the Air" but she was also known as Sud and in Assyria as Mulitu the consort of the God Enlil. She had up to seven different names depending on which location you were associating her with. She also had various parentage including the sky God Anu as her father. Her consort is Enlil who isn't generally seen in a good light by his family or the peoples who worshiped the pantheon of deities he belonged to. His brother Enki always gets the better press.

In some records Enlil is recorded as having raped Ninlil on several occasions to create all four of their children who also happen to be Gods. Two of the offspring are gods of the underworld, Nergal -Meclamta-ea and Ninazu. The third god, Enbilulu, is called the "inspector of canals".

This particular account describes Ninlil as a bit of a rebellious

young woman whose mother forbids her to bathe in the canal in Nippur but she does it anyway. The rebellious nature is also evident with Lilith and in Jewish scripture this becomes a dominant part of her personailty. Enlil sees her and is instantly aroused by the sight of her and takes her allegedly by force. Enlil didn't get away without punishment however. The Assembly of the High Council of the Gods punished him for his sex crime and he was banished to the underworld to the Goddess Ereshkigal. As he descends Ninlil follows him. It would seem that she was not entirely put off by being taken rudely by Enlil, indeed he is accredited in some texts as being thrown out of Nippur not for raping Ninlil but for coming from the lands of the dead. He is viewed as 'unclean' and therefore as a stranger or alien to their lands he is cast out. This makes more sense. One can now view it as a hasty love affair that is not approved of by Ninlils family. At the time these myths were being told in the new great cities of the area laws were being instated to ban pre-marital sex. Ninlils lack of respect for the law had him turfed out but she follows, why? Because she is pregnant. Next he is said to disguise himself as a being known as 'The Gatekeeper' whereupon he impregnates her with Nergal who goes on to be God of Death. Next is Ninizu and lastly Enbililu all Gods conceived out of wedlock. Eventually he gives in and they do seem to live relatively happily ever after. To me they are a rebellious couple escaping the wrath of outraged relatives and law makers, they are prepared to descend into the netherworld and accept it as punishment, but their love is also their salvation. But one could see where inspirations for the later Jewish Lilith of the Zohar might well have originated from stories such as these with twists being placed upon them to suit new cultures. By now Ninlil and Enlil are seen as being married. She is often described as a grain Goddess and he a God of winds. This connection could also reflect the need for pollination in nature that they both seem to fulfill. Enlil seems to be associated with the

element of water for it is said he fills his wife with water and he disguises himself once again as 'man of the river of the underworld or a man devouring river' to create the underworld God Ninazu. And finally disguising himself for the last time he manages to get away with fooling his wife once more and she conceives and delivers of Enbilulu God of rivers. Enlil has another important title and that is of God of the hoe. It is he who is held responsible for parting the heavens and the earth (Very similar to the first few days of the creation myth of Genesis in the Old Testament) and allowing seed to be sown. It is said the first hole he makes in the crust of the Earth is where mankind comes up from. Man made from dust it seems, sounds familiar. Here we have a rudimentary symbolic description of how to grow crops. You need seed, Ninlil, air to pollinate which is also Ninlil as well as Enlil and water to germinate and help the crop grow which is also Enlil.

It is also interesting that another account of Enlil and his wife Ninlil describing how the lady went from being known as Sud to Ninlil involves a less violent and aggressive sexual encounter. Here she is known as 'The lady who gives Birth' or 'The Lady who Spreads her Knees'. They are recorded as making love in sleeping quarters in a flowered bed 'fragrant like a cedar forest' and that Enlil made love to his wife and took great pleasure from it indicating a more loving union taking place. Enlil is said to say "Proud woman, surpassing the mountains! You who always fulfil your desires—from now on, Sud, Enlil is the king and Ninlil is the queen. The goddess without name has a famous name now". And it would be seen as fairly revolutionary for a man to wish to give his wife such pleasures. Taking pride in giving a woman an orgasm is still to this day seen as unnecessary in some cultures.

Here we have the birth of a Queen and a Goddess. But she was not directly considered linked with Lil-litu. Indeed they were seen as entirely different entities.

In this rather long poem, *Enlil and Ninlil* we read of their mythology as translated from Babylonian:

It was just a city, just a city
But these chose to come settle,
Nippur was just a city,
but these chose to come settle,
Durgishimmar was just a city,
but these chose to come settle.

Just Idsalla was its pure river,
just Kargeshtina its harbor quay,
just Karusar its mooring quay,
just Pulal its well of sweet water,
just Nunbirdu its shimmering canal,
if measured out, just fifty sar each
were its arable lands.

Just Enlil was its young man
just Ninlil was its young maiden
just Ninbarshegunu, was its matron.

In those days
did the mother who gave her birth
advise the girl,
Ninbarshegunu
advised Ninlil:
May you not, 'o woman,
bathe in the pure canal,
in the pure canal,
may you not 'o Ninlil,
come stepping back

unto the bank of Nunbirdu!
He who is all bright eyes,
will be laying eyes upon you,
the great mountain, father Enlil,
who is all bright eyes,
will be laying eyes upon you,
the shepherd, the decision maker,
who is all bright eyes,
will be laying eyes upon you.
Forthwith that cock
will come burgeoning
he will be kissing you
and, happy, will gladly leave with you
the glorious sperm filled into the womb.

To the mother who advised her
she on her part lent ear.
In that self same pure canal,
in that self same pure canal,
the woman came and bathed,
and Ninlil was about to come stepping
back unto the bank of Nunbirdu.

He who is all bright eyes,
the master, who is all bright eyes,
laid eyes upon her,
the great mountain, father Enlil,
who is all bright eyes,
laid eyes upon her,
the shepherd, the decision maker,
who is all bright eyes,
laid eyes upon her:

"Let me make love with you!"
he was saying to her,
but was not thereby able
to make her agree to it.
"Let me kiss you!"
Enlil was saying to her,
but was not thereby able
to make her agree to it.

"My parts are little,
know not how to stretch,
my lips are little,
know not how to kiss!
If my mother learned about it
she would be slapping my hand,
if my father learned about it,
he would be grabbing hold of me harshly,
and it would not be for me,
now, to tell my girlfriend,
I should be drying up on her!

Enlil said to his page, Nusku:
Nusku, my page!
"Yes, pray!"
Great trust of the Ekur!
"Yes, my master!"
With a girl so nice, so shapely,
with Ninlil, so nice, so shapely,
one gets an urge
to make love
one gets an urge to kiss!
  The page brought to his master

the likes of a boat
brought to him the likes of a towline
of a small boat
brought to him the likes of a big boat:
My master, willing,
let me float him down on it,
so he can follow the urge
to make that love,
follow the urge to kiss those lips,
father Enlil willing
let me float him down on it
so he can follow the urge
to make that love,
follow the urge to kiss those lips!

As he was hugging her
he held her hands,
followed the urge to kiss those lips;
and she for her part
was making lie up next to him
the bottom and the little moist place.
He followed the urge
to make that love,
followed the urge to kiss those lips,
and at his first making love,
at his first kiss,
he poured into the womb for her
the sperm, germ of Suen the moon,
the bright lone divine traveler!

Enlil was passing through Kiur,
and as Enlil was passing through Kiur

the fifty great gods,
and the seven gods
of formulating the decisions,
were seizing Enlil in Kiur:
The sex offender Enlil
will leave the town!
The sex offender Nunamnir
will leave the town!
Enlil, in accordance
with what has been decided about him,
left town.

Enlil was walking along,
Ninlil was following,
Nunamnir was walking along,
the girl was pursuing.
Enlil said to the man
in charge of the city gate:
Man of the city gate,
man of the bolt,
man of the lock,
man of the holy bolt!
Your mistress Ninlil
will be coming
an she ask you about me
do you not show her where I am!

Ninlil said to the man
in charge of the city gate:
Man of the city gate,
man of the bolt,
man of the lock,

man of the holy bolt!
Where did Enlil your master go?

Enlil had the man of the city gate answer her.

My master never deigned
to exchange pleasantries with me,
Enlil never deigned
to exchange pleasantries with me!

Having decided in my mind,
I made my plans,
and was filling from him
my empty womb,
Enlil, king of all lands
made love with me.
As Enlil is your master
so also am I your mistress!

An you be my mistress
let my hand touch your pudenda!

A sperm, your future master,
a lustrous sperm, is in my womb,
a sperm, germ of Suen the moon,
a lustrous sperm is in my womb!

May the sperm, my future master,
go heavenward,
and may my sperm
go to the netherworld,
may my sperm

instead of the sperm, my future master
come to the netherworld!

Enlil, as the man of the city gate
had her lie down in the latter's chamber,
made love with her, kissed her;
and at his lovemaking,
at his first kiss,
he poured into the womb for her
the sperm, germ of Nergal,
the one issuing forth from Meslam!

Enlil was walking along,
Ninlil was following,
Nunamnir was walking along,
the girl was pursuing.
Enlil drew near
the river of the mountains,
the man-nourishing river,
and to the man in charge
of the river of the mountains,
the man-nourishing river,
Enlil said:
Your mistress Ninlil
will be coming
an she ask you about me
do you not show her where I am!

Ninlil was nearing
the river of the mountains,
the man-nourishing river,
and to the man in charge

of the river of the mountains,
the man-nourishing river,
Ninlil said:
Where did Enlil
your master go?

Enlil had the man of the river of the mountains answer her.

My master never deigned
to exchange pleasantries with me,
Enlil never deigned
to exchange pleasantries with me!

Having decided in my mind,
I made my plans,
and was filling from him
my empty womb,
Enlil, king of all lands
made love with me.
As Enlil is your master
so also am I your mistress!
An you be my mistress
let my hand touch your pudenda!

A sperm, your future master,
a lustrous sperm, is in my womb,
a sperm, germ of Suen the moon,
a lustrous sperm is in my womb!

May the sperm, my future master,
go heavenward,
and may my sperm

go to the netherworld,
may my sperm
instead of the sperm, my future master
come to the netherworld!

Enlil, as the man in charge of the river of the mountains
had her lie down in the latter's chamber,
made love with her, kissed her;
and at his lovemaking,
at his first kiss,
he poured into the womb for her
the sperm, germ of Ninazu,
owner of the temple manor Egida!

Enlil was walking along,
Ninlil was following,
Nunamnir was walking along,
the girl was pursuing.
Enlil drew near Silulim the ferryman
Enlil said:
Your mistress Ninlil
will be coming
an she ask you about me
do you not show her where I am!

Ninlil drew near the ferryman
and said to him:
'O ferryman, where did Enlil
your master go?

Enlil had the man Silulim
make answer:

My master never deigned
to exchange pleasantries with me,
Enlil never deigned
to exchange pleasantries with me!

Having decided in my mind,
I made my plans,
and was filling from him
my empty womb,
Enlil, king of all lands
made love with me.
As Enlil is your master
so also am I your mistress!

An you be my mistress
let my hand touch your pudenda!

A sperm, your future master,
a lustrous sperm, is in my womb,
a sperm, germ of Suen the moon,
a lustrous sperm is in my womb!

May the sperm, my future master,
go heavenward,
and may my sperm
go to the netherworld,
may my sperm
instead of the sperm, my future master
come to the netherworld!

Enlil, as Silulim
had her lie down in the latter's chamber,

made love with her, kissed her;
and at his lovemaking,
at his first kiss,
he poured into the womb for her
the sperm, germ of Enbilulu,
the river warden!

Thou art lord! Thou art master!
Enlil, thou art lord! Thou art master!
Nunamnir, thou art lord! Thou art master!
A lord, carrying great weight,
lord of the storehouse,
art thou!
The lord making the barley sprout forth,
the lord making the vines sprout forth,
art thou!
Lord of heaven, lord making yields be,
and lord of the earth,
art thou!
Lord of the earth, lord making yields be,
and lord of heaven
art thou!
Enlil being lord, Enlil being master,
and inasmuch as a lord's word
cannot be changed!

Give praise unto Mother Ninlil!
Father Enlil, praise!

The comparison between this creation myth and that of the Garden of Eden has long been made. In fact it is most probably the best contender for the source of that Biblical story.

The North and South winds, Enlil and Ninlil being cast down is akin to Adam and Eve's fall from grace. Many see Lilith and Eve as two halves of the same coin once they arrive in Hebrew scripture. They fell from the sky to earth. Or from a heavenly garden to earth. A sexually related sin is committed. In this case the rape of Ninlil. Adam wanders the wilderness after his fall and Enlil wanders trying to avoid Ninlil. Death is the first born of their children, and Samael as Angel of Death is the serpent in Hebrew contexts.

Enlil was walking along, (God)
Ninlil was following, (Goddess)
Nunamnir was walking along, (Shepherd)
the girl was pursuing. (Virgin)

Here we have both the Holy deities involved in this myth relating directly with their mortal counterparts. Moving the destinies of one another as they do.

No more can they simply rely on previously easily gained fruits now they have to farm and create their own food. Which is also often cited by some ancient historians, archaeologists and anthropologists as the reason for this myth to have evolved in the first place. Making it more than a creation myth as it is the marking of the shift from hunting and gathering to partial agriculture and eventually the dominance and increased reliance on grown crops and domesticated selectively bred animals for food.

LILITH THE BABY KILLER

Of all her most feared myths it is this one. Nothing instills such terror as having the threat of losing the life of a baby. And to this day it is this one that persists the strongest. It is the main reason Jewish people don't give their girls her name. Protective amulets are still put over the cots of the newly born.

In his work *Two Thousand Years of a Charm Against the Child-Stealing Witch*, the translator T.H. Gaster mentions an amulet from the *Book of Raziel* which Gaster says is from "a compilation made in the tenth century from much older materials" but modern scholars believe it is later, around twelfth century.

I conjure thee, primitive Eve, by the name of the one who created thee, and by the names of the three angels which the Lord sent after thee, and who found thee in the islands of the sea, to whom thou didst swear, that wherever thou salt find their names neither thou nor thine host shall do any harm, also not to those who carry those names with them. I therefore conjure thee by their names and by their seals, which are written down here, that thou do no harm, neither thou, nor thy host, nor thy servants, to this woman or to the young babe to which she has given birth; neither during day-time nor during the night; neither in their food nor in their drink; neither in their head nor in their heart; nor in their 208 members, nor in their 305 veins. I conjure thee, thy hosts and thy servants, with the power of these names and these seals. (Gaster p. 153)

And so even though medical science has to a large extent managed to explain sudden infant death the fear of a Lilith attack is still alive and well in certain lands.

LAMASHTU

It is entirely possible that the source of the baby killing Lilith originated from a Sumerian Goddess known as Lamashtu. Unlike Lilith, who is also attributed with miscarriages, still born's and killing baby boys up to their circumcision and girls for up to twenty days old, Lamashtu doesn't just kill babies she is happy to feast on the flesh of men as well. But she does have a similarly terrifying reputation. The vast majority of incantations and spells to protect against Lilith are connected with her role as baby killer.

This Sumerian Goddess is often described as being a demon despite being a daughter of Anu the sky God. Stories relating to her are told in both Assyrian and Babylonian ancient texts and few are more terrifying than Lamashtu. Her name invoked one of the worst fears possible into the hearts and minds of the people of ancient Mesopotamia as she is best known for being a baby killer. She was held responsible for miscarriages, still births and the kinds of deaths that we now refer to as sudden infant death syndrome. Ancient Sumerian folklore told that she would creep into the woman's house who was either pregnant or had recently given birth and try to touch the stomach of the woman seven times in order to have her disastrous effect. She was also fond of stealing babies away from wet nurses. But she did not stop at driving terror into families this way, she also had a taste for blood and bones literally devouring her victims. And she is held responsible for spreading all manner of diseases sometimes portrayed as standing over a sick persons bed waiting for them to die. Whether her mythology evolved and as such she grew other lusts is not clear. But she does seem to have many of the more negative qualities often attributed to the Lilith myth. It is possible that parts of her story are missing and that she was a generalised Goddess of death.

She was no beauty and by all accounts often appeared as having a lion's head, teeth and sometimes the ears of a donkey, a hairy body with hands dripping in blood and long nails. She has naked breasts and the feet of an anzu bird. Yes the Anzu is back again. She is also seen holding snakes. Pazuzu, King of the wind demons,is meant to be constantly trying to push her back down into the underworld in her boat but seems to fail in his attempts. One feels they are evenly matched in strength and that an endless tension exists between them.

In his book *Lilith the First Eve* Seigmund Hurwitz makes the connection and explores it at length drawing heavily from the

ancient Babylonion Lambartu Texts that DW Myhrman has since published. These texts describe Lamashtu who is otherwise known as Lambartu thus;

"Her abode is on the mountains, or in the reed beds. Dreadful is her appearance. Her head and her face are those of a fearsome lion, white as clay is her countenance, she has form of an ass, from her lips pours spittle, she roars like a lion, she howls like a jackal. A whore is she. Fearsome and savage is her nature. Raging furious, fearsome, terrifying, violent, rapacious, evil, malicious, she overthrows and destroys all she approaches. Terrible are her deeds. Wherever she comes, wherever she appears, she brings evil and destruction. Men, beasts, trees, rivers, roads, buildings, she brings harm to them all. A flesh eating, bloodsucking monster is she."

Though in a tension with her, Pazuzu is often the one petitioned to protect against Lamashtu. He commanded and controlled the south west wind known for its ferocity and ability to bring droughts and famines. He is usually portrayed as having the head of a lion with a man's body, wings, feet of an eagle, a tail like a scorpion and, most importantly, a snake-like penis. Bronze heads of Pazuzu were worn by women anxious to be safe from his rival Lamashtu. Although demonic he had the power to protect against other demons.

Offerings of centipedes sometimes placated her as did carved stones and metal brooches. Many incantations otherwise known as 'shiptu' were read over any person thought to be afflicted by this demon or Goddess though she is often seen as part of a group of demons named the Uttuke. Charms, amulets, are used in order to both protect and exorcize the effects of a suspected Lamashtu attack. One such ritual that was carried out included bringing a black dog carrying the effigy of Lamashtu over which bread and water are offered up, this is put near the afflicted person for three days with the heart of a piglet in its mouth. Incantations and further offerings are made during this period and at dusk on the third day

the figure is removed and buried by a wall. This Akkadian practise was common of similar rituals for banishing demonic forces and is akin to many others found all over Sumer.

Those of you reading this book who are on the Lilith current today will, no doubt, already be picking up on the elements and attributes of the Jewish Lilith to come and the one most people are more familiar with. There is no doubt in my mind that the family of Lil-litu, the Goddess Ninlil and the Queen of Demons Lamashtu have all played a part in her composition.

Yet another example of the belief in Lilith's baby killing attributes was found on a 7th century text found on a magical amulet from Syria found in Arslan Tash describes Lilith as *"O flyer in a dark chamber Go away at once O lili!"* This is a segment of an incantation said over pregnant women in childbirth. On one side is a winged human with a lion's head standing over a wolf with a scorpion's tail that is devouring a human being. On the reverse is a marching God carrying an axe, possibly Gilgamesh. But modern day scholars dispute this as being a reference to the Jewish Lilith.

THE GILGAMESH CONTROVERSY

To find yet more of the roots of this Lilith we return to Mesopotamia and this time to the *Epic of Gilgamesh*. Gilgamesh is mentioned in the list of Sumerian Kings as being the fifth king of the first dynasty of Uruk which was roughly 2,700-2,500 BCE. And as already mentioned his father was Alu a wind demon. Thought to have been written around 2,400 BCE it contains the first recorded reference to Lilith. The fact she is mentioned incidentally almost as if she needed no explanation and therefore was well known has been noted by many scholars interested in her. The poem was written on twelve tablets over a period of about 1,500 years indicating the tradition was oral until the arrival of writing during

the third dynastic period. But this poem wasn't originally a part of the great Epic which contains one of the most accurate descriptions of the great flood ever recorded. It was first told as *Gilgamesh and the Huluppu Tree* or otherwise known as *Bilgames and the Netherworld* but some of it was missing so they added it to the Epic. Although this poem has already seeped into the consciousness of modern day Lilith devotees it is not generally accepted as being reliable as a genuine source of true Lilith material by serious academics. Arguments over translations are best left to academics of which I am not. But, the name in the original poem that is meant to relate to Lilith is *Ki-sikil-lil-la-ke* the maiden who screeches but is a gladdener of hearts, and according to Siegmund Hurwitz there is another name often found with this one *Ki-sikil-ud-da-kar-ra*, the maiden who stole or seized the light. Both of these have some Lilith qualities.

In this ancient excerpt from the Gilgamesh poem to Inanna, as translated by Samuel Noah Kramer Lilith is mentioned as a demon or maiden depending on which translation you prefer.

After heaven and earth had been separated
and mankind had been created,
after Anu, Enlil and Ereskigal had taken possession
of heaven, earth and the underworld;
after Enki had set sail for the underworld
and the sea ebbed and flowed in honor of its lord;
on this day, a huluppu tree
which had been planted on the banks of the Euphrates
and nourished by its waters
was uprooted by the south wind
and carried away by the Euphrates.
A goddess who was wandering among the banks
seized the swaying tree

And – at the behest of Anu and Enlil –
brought it to Inanna's garden in Uruk.
Inanna tended the tree carefully and lovingly
she hoped to have a throne and a bed
made for herself from its wood.
After ten years, the tree had matured.
But in the meantime, she found to her dismay
that her hopes could not be fulfilled.
because during that time
a dragon had built its nest at the foot of the tree
the Zu-bird was raising its young in the crown,
and the demon Lilith had built her house in the middle.
But Gilgamesh, who had heard of Inanna's plight,
came to her rescue.
He took his heavy shield
killed the dragon with his heavy bronze axe,
which weighed seven talents and seven minas.
Then the Zu-bird flew into the mountains
with its young,
while Lilith, petrified with fear,
tore down her house and fled into the wilderness

In a subsequent translation with Wolkstein, this passage is
given as:

... a serpent who could not be charmed
made its nest in the roots of the tree,
The Anzu bird set his young in the branches of the tree,
And the dark maid Lilith built her home in the trunk.
If it were an academically accurate and accepted translation then
it certainly places Lilith as being in existence at the birth of creation.

In fact it seems to imply that she was there all along even before these supposed creation deities had done with their initial work. Yet again she is both before and after. She is sometimes depicted with dark skin which could well be what Wolkstein felt the text pertained to. But some will say it is her nature which is considered 'dark' or negative and destructive. Many see Lilith as both extremes in character and appearance either as a Nubian black skinned beauty or a milk skinned one. To those on her current she often appears in both guises and others besides and her ability to be destructive is balanced out by her ability to be creative. And if darkness is to be interpreted another way it might simply mean she is hidden from view or her true nature obscured.

The Zu bird is often a storm bird and could well be the Anzu bird yet again. This bird seems to be very much evident in all her possible connections. The south wind is controlled by Ninlil and so she must have a part to play in this and the dragon at the base is also translated as a snake which is associated with Lamashtu and Lilith. And yet it is Inanna who is the Goddess seemingly demoted in this poem. The huluppu tree is Sumerian for a white willow. This very thirsty individual often grows alongside rivers. Willow have long associations in Sumerian and other cultures with eternity and immortality. As well as the obvious health benefits they can give us in the form of herbal medicine they are also capable of constant regrowth. Usually where ever you find one there has probably always been one. Even an apparent dead willow can throw new shoots that root very easily and quickly. Like many I find them amazing and magical and it is no wonder many of our ancestors did also. They are frequently connected to the underworld or world of the dead. Snakes can also live on all levels. They have nests underground which many of the ancient peoples including the Sumerians equated with the world of the dead. Plus they bask by day in the sun and can easily slither up trees looking for food and warmth so they can exist

above with the Gods, at ground level with us and in the underworld with the dead. If you add the ability to shed skin and survive you have another link with apparent immortality. The zu bird or anzu bird was most likely an eagle and my favourite contender for this position is the eagle owl. Eagles rarely nest in trees they prefer remote rocky outcrops or ledges of mountains and cliffs. Owls however do. And an eagle owl is a very large one, especially a Middle Eastern one, often standing at three foot plus with a six foot wingspan the Middle Eastern Eagle Owl is an incredibly impressive bird. And yes it could definitely take on small children if it wished to although it would be unlikely if other food was available. Here we seem to have an image of a tree nurtured by an existing well respected Goddess, Inanna, and suddenly invaded by all manner of beings she is unable to get rid of. Only Gilgamesh can rid her of the incumbents.

Here is an early translation of the tale, as told by Samuel Noah Kramer in 1944. The beginning does seem to imply this was a story repeatedly told. Kramer's translation has since been thrown into dispute.

Once upon a time there was a huluppu-tree, perhaps a willow; it was planted on the banks of the Euphrates; it was nurtured by the waters of the Euphrates. But the South Wind tore at it, root and crown, while the Euphrates flooded it with its waters. Inanna, queen of heaven, walking by, took the tree in her hand and brought it to Erech, the seat of her main sanctuary, and planted it in her holy garden. There she tended it most carefully. For when the tree grew big, she planned to make of its wood a chair for herself and a couch.

Years passed, the tree matured and grew big. But Inanna found herself unable to cut down the tree. For at its base the snake 'who knows no charm' had built its nest. In its crown, the Zu-bird – a mythological creature which at times wrought mischief -- had placed its young. In the middle Lilith, the maid of desolation, had built her

house. And so poor Inanna, the light-hearted and ever-joyful maid, shed bitter tears. And as the dawn broke and her brother, the sun-god Utu, arose from his sleeping chamber, she repeated to him tearfully all that had befallen her huluppu-tree.

Now Gilgamesh, the great Sumerian hero, the forerunner of the Greek Heracles, who lived in Erech, overheard Inanna's weeping complaint and chivalrously came to her rescue. He donned his armor weighing fifty minas – about fifty pounds – and with his 'ax of the road,' seven talents and seven minas in weight – over four hundred pounds – he slew the snake 'who knows no charm' at the base of the tree. Seeing which, the Zu-Bird fled with his young to the mountain, and Lilith tore down her house and fled to the desolate places which she was accustomed to haunt. The man of Erech who had accompanied Gilgamesh now cut down the tree and presented it to Inanna for her chair and couch.

FOR ERECH READ URUK

This precursor to the soon to become Jewish Lilith is also heavily weaved into the myth of the Garden of Eden which is covered in its own chapter. But when we look at the imagery we have a maid Lilith who is seemingly a free and independent spirit making her home in a holy garden in the tree saved by a Goddess. Her companions the bird and the snake seem quite at peace with her and yet invoke great fear in the great Goddess Inaana who cannot rid herself of them. Only the axe of the King Gilgamesh (This King was said to be of one third divine blood) can banish Lilith and her friends. It seems as though great peace dwelt in the tree and was replaced by fear and destruction.

I asked Her, "what of this poem?" and it seemed to me that She answered:

"My serpent that will not be tamed is your primal nature. Inaana wept at seeing it, in the raw it fills all with fear. The owl flew, as did I, for our home was taken from us." she laughs. "Out with the old and in with the new, desolation, awaits all"

The Babylonians who destroyed the Temple at Jerusalem in 587 BCE would have known of the Lili and Lilu. They would have known of Lamashtu and of Ardat-lili and Lil-litu. The exiled, enslaved and displaced Israelites were forced to walk the perilous journey to Babylon and many stayed there until 539BCE when conditions were more favorable for some to return to Judah. But the forty or so years that many experienced living in Ur would have meant that some attended schools and were educated in the local language and heard the Persian, Sumerian and Akkadian myths. These obviously had a profound effect on these Hebrew peoples as many found their way into Judaic mythology and eventually became part of the Old Testament. And this is possibly the time that had the greatest influence on the migration of Lilith to the land of Israel.

THE BURNEY RELIEF

This ancient artifact (see cover) stands alone in its own cabinet in the Mesopotamian section of the British Museum. It has been and still is subject of much debate and disagreement. It is thought to have originated from Southern Iraq (which definitely places it in Sumer) and is believed to have been created around 1800-1750 BCE. It is named The Burney Relief after Sidney Burney an antiquities dealer who acquired it from a Syrian in the 1920's. The British Museum obviously rates it quite highly in their exhibits having paid about £1,500,000 for it. It depicts a nude female form with wings in a downward position. On her head appears to be a crown of four horns with a disc above and in each hand she holds a rod and hoop.

Her feet are bird's talons and she stands upon what is thought to be two lions. Either side of the lions are two owls. From traces of the original paint it seems that the background was once black, the lady herself has red skin, her wings are red, black and white and she is adorned with golden jewelry. This hardly seems an image of a demon. Called simply 'Queen of the Night' she has several possible identities. Some say she is Ishtar, some Ereshikgal and some Inaana but many also declare her as Lilith. I cannot prove this image is Lilith any more it seems than the academics can. And yet I know from experience that Lilith is quite happy to be seen as it.

It is generally believed to have been used in ritual and might have been a focal point for a cult who worked with The Queen of the Night. I like this title and feel it a good compromise for an otherwise hotly debated identity. Similar artwork and styles have been excavated at Nippur, Ur, Isin and Larsa. It is in keeping with the late Babylonian period. The horned crown with central disc is found elsewhere as are images similar to this one on vases. They usually pertain to royalty and divine status. Lions are also occasionally found alongside deities but only this one has owls. There are images of Inaana and Ishtar that are similar but not identical which in my mind makes this one unique. In my own research with my limited sources and my personal link with Lilith, this screams of herself. Placed as being found when the area concerned was in turmoil it wouldn't surprise me if a small Lilith cult commissioned the relief purely to invoke Herself and protect them from invaders. It has also been suggested that the relief might have been in a brothel due to the nudity but this is fairly unlikely. The colours of her wings fascinate me, for you find red, black and white frequently associated with goddesses all over the world in a variety of cultures and traditions. And although fans of the Erekshigal theory favour the black representing the underworld the museum seems to have fallen on the side of it being a sign of the night time. And as neither

Inaana or Ishtar are usually seen with owls and Lilith has, if you believe at least one of the translations of the Gilgamesh and the Huluppu Tree and the reference in Isaiah to what could be Lilith as a shriek owl then to me it is still open to discussion. And until another like it is found with Her name, I doubt it will ever be truly resolved.

CHAPTER TWO

THE JEWISH LILITH

B y the time that Lilith embeds herself in the Jewish scriptures she has become a complex being. The Lilith we meet now has many facets and a very sophisticated personality. Her energy has grown substantially from what might have begun as a raw wind demon to succubus, demoness, vampire, Goddess and now enters the arena of Judaism. In some respects one could say to really understand this Lilith you need to get your head into the mindset of Judaism in its early days up until modern day. She appears in many well-known texts such as The Zohar, Talmud and assorted Rabbinic scriptures and literature. I have attempted to narrow this down as much as possible to the main areas she manifests in, starting with the etymology of her name.

In Hebrew Lilith is usually *lyl* or *layil* meaning originating from the Semitic word for 'night'. Charles Fossey in 1902 translated Lilith as meaning *'female night being/demon'* and whereas the Akkadian *lili* and *Lilitu* mean 'spirits', *lilu* means 'evening'. In Sumerian *lil* simply means air. So her most potent time is night and those who work with Lilith will all agree her energy kicks in as the sun sets. Although very much an Earth demon her main element is air and she is certainly one for stirring up storms. But air is the element traditionally viewed as being associated with thought and communication in esoteric terms so she is able to use this to get into our minds. In most Jewish sources she is essentially a female demonic spirit. In absolute bare essence this is an intelligent female spiritual demonic energy that awakes at night. As to how she

behaves or reacts, well that can be potentially any extreme.

I began by looking at the most well-known Biblical reference. But like most evidence to date, even this is tenuous and not entirely proven to be relating to Lilith. In some versions 'Night Hag' is mentioned in others Lilith and some bare no mention to either. But it is in Isaiah 34:13-15 and a list of eight unclean animals that may have demonic qualities that she is sometimes found. In this description of the desolation of Edom the eight are sometimes referred to as one.

(12) Her nobles shall be no more, nor shall kings be proclaimed there; all her princes are gone. (13) Her castles shall be overgrown with thorns, her fortresses with thistles and briers. She shall become an abode for jackals and a haunt for ostriches. (14) Wildcats shall meet with desert beasts, satyrs shall call to one another; There shall the Lilith repose, and find for herself a place to rest. (15) There the hoot owl shall nest and lay eggs, hatch them out and gather them in her shadow; There shall the kites assemble, none shall be missing its mate. (16) Look in the book of the LORD and read: No one of these shall be lacking, For the mouth of the LORD has ordered it, and His spirit shall gather them there. (17) It is He who casts the lot for them, and with His hands He marks off their shares of her; They shall possess her forever, and dwell there from generation to generation.

And the King James Version relates it slightly more succinctly;

The wild cat shall meet with the jackals
And the satyr shall cry to his fellow
And Lilith shall find repose there
And find her a place of rest

This refers to the alleged time when the leaders of Edom (Judah)

refused access through their lands to the Jews during their exodus from Egypt. Jeremiah's prophecy from 'The Lord' is their response to the Edomites. This description of the Jews threat upon Edom states that once they are done with these lands only wild 'unclean' creatures will survive there. All of the House of Esua were to die. The unclean usually consisted of creatures they considered unsuitable as food. "Her castles, Her nobles etc." applies to Edom as a daughter of Babylon, it was frequently described in the feminine, a little like we call cars women so they often referred to their 'people' and cities in the feminine. The Babylonians and Edomites were allies at this time. They wish Edom to become a desolate wasteland fit only for filth and death and decay and, Lilith, their ultimate threat. To them she was the most feared of all spirits, she will 'find her repose' indicating it will be a place only a being such as Lilith could possibly be at rest in. In other words she will be in her evil element once God deals out this judgement against them. And so here we have ancient texts that directly link Lilith with such energies as are often found when connecting with her today.

THE ZOHAR/KABBALAH

A place drawn heavily from by today's Western Mystery Schools and many occultists who work with Lilith is the Zohar. It is a complex body of work that explores the more mystical side of Judaism. The main two books included in it are The Book of Creation or Sefer Yetzirah and The Book of Radiance or Bahir. Put in the simplest way possible the first covers the mystical message from God in Genesis and the second is gnostic in nature and helps guide the student inwards towards their own divinity. The entire contents are most probably sourced from all manner of texts, scrolls, oral traditions etc from Babylonia to Talmudic, and might well include knowledge from a great variety of older ancient paths and traditions. It also draws heavily from the five books of Moses or Tanakh. Studying the

Zohar is rejected by some Orthodox Hassidic Jews and embraced by others. The Zohar is thought to have originated from various Rabbanic Midrash's put together throughout a period between 539 BCE and 70 CE. The first Rabbi believed to have put what many claim was an oral tradition to paper in was Rabbi Simeon Bar Yohai. But he claimed direct lineage from Adam and wisdom imparted to him from God. The full compilation of twenty two volumes was written around 1200 CE in Spain by Rabbi Moses de Leon. There are some that say Rabbi Moses de Leon was the only person responsible for creating it but it is unlikely that he could have put such a body of work together in the time frame allowed and the differences in grammar etc. lean towards it being a compilation of earlier scriptures. But either way it is compelling spiritual mysticism that has survived and been a source of wisdom and inspiration ever since its creation.

The Tree of Life contains greater secrets than the Tree of Knowledge which according to Genesis taught Adam and Eve the difference between good and evil. The Tree of Life remains in the Garden after man's fall from grace and is guarded by flames or cherubim. The Adam lineage we all have, in theory according to those who believe such things, would contain within it the ancestral memory of this knowledge. The Kabbalah reveals these secrets. But the flip side to the Tree of Life is the Tree of Death or the Qliphoth. Here we also find Lilith. Death being equated with evil, and the necessity of it being part of 'God' its presence shielding the pure divine source.

LILITH IN THE ZOHAR

The Zohar claims Lilith was created at the same time as Adam from dust just as he was. It goes on further to say she rose up from spirits that gave her life, some translations say she came from the abyss or void and some others say it pertains to the depths of the

oceans. All agree she rose up. She is mentioned in the Zohar no less than fifty six times which considering how little she appears in the Tanakh is quite incredible. It also agrees that she failed to be a suitable partner for Adam or 'helpmate' as is often cited.

Zohar 1:19b

After the primeval light was hidden, a husk was created for the brain, and that husk spread out and brought forth another husk which was Lilith. And when she emerged, she went up and went down towards the little faces, and wanted to attach herself to them and be shaped after them, and did not want to depart from them. But the Holy One, blessed be He, removed her from there and placed her down below. When He created Adam, in order to perfect this world, as soon as Lilith saw Eve affixed to the side of Adam, and saw in them the beauty of the Above, and saw their perfect image, she flew off from there and wanted, as before to attach herself to the little faces. But the guardians of the gates of Above did not Let her. The Holy One, blessed be He, rebuked her, and cast her into the depths of the sea, and she remained dwelling there until Adam and his wife sinned. Then the Holy One, blessed be He, brought her up from the depths of the sea and gave her power over all those children, the little faces of the sons of man, who are liable to punishment because of the sins of their fathers. And she went and roamed the world. She approached the gates of Paradise on earth, and saw the Cherubim guarding the gates of Paradise, and sat down facing the Flaming Sword, for she originated from that flame. When that flame revolved, she fled. And she roams in the world, and finds children liable to punishment, and caresses them, and kills them. And all this is because of the diminishing of the moon which reduced its light. When Cain was born, she could not attach herself to him. But later she approached him and bore spirits and winged demons. For 130 years Adam had intercourse with female spirits,

until Naamah came. Because of her beauty the sons of God went astray after her, 'Ussa and 'Azael, and she bore from them, and from her spread evil. spirits and demons in the world . . . And she goes and roams the world at night, and makes sport with men and causes them to emit seed. And wherever men are found sleeping alone in a house, they [these spirits] descend upon them and get hold of them and adhere to them and take desire from them and bear from them. And they also afflict them with disease, and the men do not know it. And all this is because of the diminishing of the moon.

This pretty much describes the Lilith most are familiar with today. She appears to be the primordial darkness, the night time, the time of false light as in the moon. And is the rebellious independent spirit who is cast down for rejecting Adam and cannot have sex in a normal manner. She can only give birth to demons/spirits and is a threat to mortal children and men. Most of the modern day Lilith qualities are mentioned here. But an added quality has been given, that of being the husk or shell of God, she who covers him and protects us all from being blinded by his/her light. And finally has her lunar link, the waning moon.

This transcript elaborates even further into the Lilith myth. It seems as though the writer wishes us to see she was born almost as soon as the universe itself. This definitely places her creation in the spiritual minds of this time as a creatrix. She goes up and attaches herself to the little faces, or souls of man. Here we have an alternative story with Adam and Eve. Lilith is sent 'below' and sees the Edenic couple and yet still she prefers to return to the 'little faces' she draws her energy from mankind. The guardians of the angelic realms refuse her entry and she is cast into the sea by 'God'. Here there could be a link with the great dragon Leviathon another fallen angel, this aspect of Lilith is rarely mentioned and yet it could well be one of her earliest primeval manifestations. She dwells

under the sea until Adam and Eve sin. It then transpires that she is brought up out of her watery abyss to punish the children of Adam and Eve for their sins and is held responsible for their suffering and premature deaths. This taking us back to Lamashtu and the Lil-itu demonic family yet again. Then out of left field we have a reference to Lilith's flame, something modern day Lilith devotees are very familiar with. It is said here that she sits in front of the flame and that this flame is also her but when it revolves she flees. It invokes primal fear into her, more on this in chapter 5. We also read on to find out that the time associated with Lilith's destructive powers is the waning moon; this time is often associated with banishing and purging etc by today's modern witches but the waning moons energy is often one that becomes creepier as it wanes, the energy is hard to describe but the lessening light and the gradual plunge into the total darkness of the dark moon was a time of mystery, foreboding, and often linked with onsets of disease in ancient folklore.

Following this Cain is mentioned and although she tries, Lilith cannot attach herself to him. Although not mentioned in this excerpt Cain is often believed to be the product of Eve and Samael, Samael being one of Lilith's consorts, often described as her twin soul or flame. Cain the rejected by God and one who murdered his own brother, Abel, out of rage and jealousy appeals to Lilith. She is a fallen one, rejected by God, and so is her magical son. Incest apart, she seems to succeed at possessing her offspring and enjoys making demons with him. Now this might well have been borrowed from the Egyptian tradition and reflects the mythos of Asur/Osiris and Sutekh/Set.

Adam is supposed to have abandoned Eve after their ejection from paradise and roamed the world copulating with spirits. But Naamah is also a name for the lesser or younger Lilith often seen as her daughter. Along with three other sisters she is considered an angel of sacred prostitution. She visits Adam as a succubi and has

his demonic children. Often cited as a gardener and lady of flowers she is also seen as a psychopomp, necromancer and medium. Linked with the element of earth she is closer to us in some respects than Lilith and not quite as frightening. It is written here that it was she who led the Gods astray. Note here it is Gods plural and not angels as in the fallen variety. And here Naamah is accredited with causing the ones known as Ussa and Azael to fall from grace by copulating with her. These are generally thought to be angels. However, I have found reference to a Goddess with a similar name called Uzza who is a Goddess. Naamah now takes on the role of succubus and is also linked with the power of the waning moon. Naamah seems to be also held responsible for sexually transmitted diseases. So this is a lady of mixed fortunes. But cures for STD's were probably thin on the ground back then so it follows that prostitutes were held more responsible for spreading them.

The Zohar 2:264b accuses Lilith of being the one held responsible for creating childhood diphtheria. This horrendous disease is rarely seen in the developed world today and yet once was quite prolific. Caused by an upper respiratory infection those afflicted develop a thickened leathery neck and eventually their airway closes and they die of asphyxiation. As those with it often describe having it as if a serpent or snake was strangling them one can see why Lilith/Samael get labelled with causing this illness. In mainstream Orthodox Judaism Samael is first mentioned as an Arch Angel, the Angel of Death. Both Lilith and Samael are held responsible for bringing death into the world. In reading and identifying with this myth one can see where much of today's Lilith knowledge and mysteries have come from. But this is not the end, oh no far from it.

Zohar 1:34b

When the letters of the name of Adam, descended below, together in their completeness, the male and the female were found

together, and the female was attached to his side, until God cast a deep slumber upon him and he fell asleep. And he lay in the place of the Temple below. And the Holy One, blessed be He, sawed her off him, and adorned her as they adorn a bride, and brought her to him . . .

This reference to the splitting of the male and female is found time and time again in Jewish mysticism. The concept that each soul splits into two half's to experience separate sexual identities and experiences and can only be 'whole' if joined with its pair is common in Judaism and also survives to this day in various branches of Christian mysticism. But the duality does not sit well with monotheism.

Zohar 3:19

Come and see: There is a female, a spirit of all spirits, and her name is Lilith, and she was at first with Adam. And in the hour when Adam was created and his body became completed, a thousand spirits from the left [evil] side clung to that body until the Holy One, blessed be He, shouted at them and drove them away. And Adam was lying, a body without a spirit, and his appearance was green, and all those spirits surrounded him. In that hour a cloud descended and pushed away all those spirits. And when Adam stood up, his female was attached to his side. And that Holy Spirit which was in him spread out to this side and that side, and grew here and there, and thus became complete. Thereafter the Holy One, blessed be He, sawed Adam into two, and made the female. And He brought her to Adam in her perfection like a bride to the canopy. When Lilith saw this, she fled. And she is in the cities of the sea, and she is still trying to harm the sons of the world.

'A spirit of all spirits' this is quite some title. It leads many Lilith devotees to see her as the ultimate or highest of all spirits. It also

states that according to this observance she was the first woman. The thousand spirits attached to Adams left side might well have been created by Lilith but it doesn't say. The initial emphasis is on making Adam 'pure' and 'whole' balanced and androgynous. It is also unclear as to whether the green appearance of Adam has any spiritual relevance, one can read into this many things. So he lays there, soulless and green with the spirits previously attached to his left side still swirling around him until a divine cloud blows them away from him. The next part is not clear however, is the female half of him Lilith? Or Eve? Eve isn't mentioned and we know Lilith flees so one could presume it is her but the mention of her 'seeing the bride and fleeing' seems to indicate that the bride is not Lilith but Eve. She goes to the 'cities of the sea' this is interesting as if we take it literally then there are many drowned cities. Genesis mentions the Red Sea as her domain.

The story is repeated, each time given a slightly difference inference. The left hand side being evil is still seen that way in the Middle East. The right is used for eating and writing the left for wiping ones posterior. The right side is masculine and good the left feminine and evil. Hence sorcery and witchcraft being a left hand path by and large.

In Zohar 1:20a (Bereshit: Passage 109)
"Let there be lights (me'orot), everything derives from it. It also includes the creation of Lilit in the world." The light or lights that create all life, stars, allow for Lilith. They contrast the husk or darkness that shields the light and gives space for death and decay.

At the end of Zohar 1:19b The defective light or flame that Lilith turns from is often seen as Samael, she flees from his side indicating they split into two halves just as Yahweh and Asherah do. This light is also accredited as being the waning moons light a light that is fading and diminishing. The two husks or shells of Lilith (Lilith

the elder and younger) provide a home for Samael to reside in. And so although they are no longer one being they still work together and can also separate by virtue of the fact Lilith and Naamah can work together or independently allowing Samael to be with either of them and therefore always active.

Zohar 1:148a-148b (Vayetze: Passage 23). Here Lilith is called the *"female of Samael,"* whom is Lucifer. Here we read; *"Samael is like the soul and Lilith like the body. Deeds are wrought by Lilith with the power of Samael."* Here the light is Samael and the physical vessel is Lilith which seems at odds with the Eden description earlier. And yet it is not. The ability to utilise the power of the divine, Holy Spirit resides in both Lilith and Samael. The diminishing light being both the waning light of death and the moon.

1:148a-148b (Vayetze: Passage 23) *One shape emerged (from both), made of male and female (Good and Evil), as one. The male is called "Samael", and his female is always included with him. Just as on the side of holiness there are male and female, so on "the other side" there are male and female, included one with the other. The female of Samael is called "snake", "a wife of harlotry", "the end of all flesh", "the end of days". Two evil spirits are attached to one another. The male spirit is fine, the female spirit spreads out down several ways and paths, and is attached to the male spirit.*

And so where the 'light' side of the Tree relates to God and his Matronit or Shekina, usually seen as Asherah the last Hebrew Goddess (Much of the Zohar relates to how the reciting of the Torah helps rise the Shekina to Yahweh and how it is every practising Jews responsibility to help do this as part of their spiritual duty) the 'other side' houses Lilith and Samael who bring the 'end of days' or death. The female snake could well be a reference to diptheria as

it is interesting that they describe the female of Samael as 'snake', this word is masculine in Hebrew. The comment 'wife of harlotry' often gets mentioned in relation to Lilith both as a sign of her role as a sacred prostitute and one who happily commits adultery or encourages and inspires people to. Samael is still an acceptable side of 'God' death being a necessity at this level of the Garden (The Garden of Eden is a multi-level plane of existence in the Zohar our plane being the lowest life exists on) and is described as 'fine' where as the female spirit, Lilith, can spread herself in all directions. This also ties up with the concept of Samael being the 'blind God' he is 'fine' or can only move or see through Lilith.

And finally from the Zohar we have 2:xxx (Pekudei: Passage 454)

When Adam was in the Garden of Eden and was occupied in worshipping his Master, Samael went down with all the grades in him, and was riding on the evil serpent to deviate them. As the serpent underneath was subtle, and led astray and seduced people, as it is written, "For the lips of a strange woman drip honey, and her mouth is smoother than oil"

(Mishlei 5:3). He gives power and she practices the art (of seduction and instigation) in the world, and they cannot rule the one without the other.

Here Samael 'rides the serpent' he and Lilith use their combined sexual energy to enter the garden and make themselves known to Adam. 'The lips of a strange woman dripping honey', could be seen as a term describing Eve becoming aroused or reference to Lilith appearing along with, 'the serpent', and being seductive and sickly sweet. Samael and Lilith are the sexual energy, the original sin, the apple moment.

Moses ben Solomon of Burgos writes;

Lilith is called the Northerner, because: "Out of the north the evil breaks forth" (Jer. 1:14). Why North is the direction from which evil breaks forth isn't explained. But many use this direction when

working with Lilith. To me North can also related to the ground under our feet and to see Lilith rise up as a female form from impure sediment or dust (dust of the dead) makes sense.

Both Samael, king of the demons, and Lilith were born in a spiritual birth androgynously. The Tree of Knowledge of Good and Evil is an epithet for both Samael and Grandmother Lilith (e.g. the Northerner). As a result of Adam's sin, both of them came and confused the whole world, both the Upper one and the Nether one.

The upper meaning Heaven and the nether meaning Earth. Though Samael is not usually named as King of Demons that title is usually reserved for Asmoday/Asmodeus/Ashmodai.

Bacharach, Emeq haMelekh 23c-d

Zohar Sitre Torah 1:148a-b

And the Serpent, the Woman of Harlotry, incited and seduced Eve through the husks of Light which in itself is holiness. And the Serpent seduced Holy Eve, and enough said for him who understands. An all this ruination came about because Adam the first man coupled with Eve while she was in her menstrual impurity -- this is the filth and the impure seed of the Serpent who mounted Eve before Adam mounted her. Behold, here it is before you: because of the sins of Adam the first man all the things mentioned came into being. For Evil Lilith, when she saw the greatness of his corruption, became strong in her husks, and came to Adam against his will, and became hot from him and bore him many demons and spirits and Lilin. (Patai 81:455f).

This description of the seduction of Eve causes confusion at best but, if you consider it possible that Lilith took the form of Samael to do the seducing and in so doing caused Eve to have her first menstrual cycle it makes more sense. So Cain is conceived by Lilith and Samael during menses, and Adam then takes his wife at this time which leads onto the tradition upheld to this day among many Jews that it is an unclean time and women are not to have sex then.

By getting to both Adam and Eve first and contaminating them with death and disease Lilith and Samael made sure their own seed was embedded in the future of mankind and that they would have to deal with the consequences for ever more. Cain was this result.

But at the same time it also says that the 'husks of light which in itself is holiness' is the vehicle for this coupling. My humble understanding of this is that Lilith provided the 'Holy Spirit' and Samael the physical means by which to impregnate Eve.

Zohar Lilith - Harlot / Whore

This passage from the Zohar 148a-148b Sitrei Torah portrays her manner of being towards men.

The *secret* of secrets: *From the strength of the noon-flame of Isaac (Geburah), from the wine lees, a naked shoot came forth, comprising together male and female, red like a lily, and they spread out on several sides, down several paths. The male is called "Samael," [literally: "the bitter beverage of God"] and his female [Lilith] is always included with him. Just as on the side of holiness there are male and female, so on 'the other side' there are male and female, included one with the other. The female of Samael is called 'snake,' 'a wife of harlotry,' 'the end of all flesh,' 'the end of days.' Two evil spirits are attached to one another. The male spirit is fine, the female spirit spreads out down several ways and paths, and is attached to the male spirit.*

The above we have already covered but is interesting to follow how this text continues.

She adorns herself with many ornaments like a despicable harlot, and takes up her position at the cross-roads to seduce the sons of man. When a fool approaches her, she grabs him, kisses him, pours him wine of dregs of vipers gall.

It is Lilith's nature to seduce, she is dominant sexually, she is also promiscuous and prefers to break up or cause strife to relationships so is often the hidden inspiration for many of these things. Her choice to play this role is her nature, she is the unbridled one. And so she prays on men who might cross her path, those starved of sex, ones who want secret liaisons, those who seek prostitutes, and she always knows exactly what arouses each of her prey. The dregs of vipers gall often refers to her kiss, it is poison, he may fall for her charms but they will cause him grief in the end. And whether this is merely in her role as succubus or by inspiring one of her 'children' (A theory I go into in more depth in a later chapter) is unclear.

The English Occultist and writer Andrew Chumbley describes this as the cross roads meant by the description of Lilith's behaviour in the Zohar. He felt he met her here and through deliberate replication of the trance like self hypnotic state of being was able to gain a direct channel to her. And is usually this state of being that provides the portal for succubus and incubus to enter through.

As soon as he drinks it he goes astray after her. When she sees that he has gone astray after her, from the path of truth (truth being love) she divests herself of all ornaments which she put on for that fool. Her ornaments for the sons of man are, her hair is long and red like a rose, her cheeks are white and red, from her ears hang six ornaments, Egyptian chords and all the ornaments from the land of the East hang from her nape. Her mouth is set like a narrow door, comely in its décor, her tongue is sharp like a sword, her words are smooth like oil. She is dressed in scarlet and adorned with forty ornaments less one. Yon fool goes astray after her and drinks from the cup of wine and commits with her fornication, and strays after her. What does she thereupon do? She leaves him asleep. Flies up to the heavens, denounces him, takes her leave and descends.

Although the literal description of her 'adornments' and clothing etc were relevant when this text was written in truth it can still apply only in so far as she dresses to provoke sexual interest. Once she knows she has the heart of her victim she loses interest in him. Her aim being purely to encourage him to go astray from his previous path.

That fool awakens and deems he can make sport with her as before, but she removes her ornaments and becomes a menacing figure. She stands before him clothed in garments of flaming fire, inspiring terror and making body and soul tremble. Full of frightening eyes holding a sword dripping poison she kills the fool and casts him into Gehenna. (Hell)

Plus once she knows she has accomplished her mission she shows her true nature to him. This being of the terrifying opposite of the women he has fallen for.

This seems a warning against adultery and seeking prostitutes for men but it is way more than this. Between the lines lays Lilith's free spirited nature. She isn't after a mans soul or his heart she merely wants to entice him out of his bounds. To me she is the sexual liberator. She has her twin flame, she is possessed by Samael and he by her, she doesn't need or want the souls of men to fall for her. She likes to cause chaos and break down forms including relationships or so it seems but one could also say she comes at times when such things are under strain and her arrival marks a turning point in the man's life. A marriage counselor she is not! But a powerful sexually liberating female she most definitely is! To me it is as if she knows if the man has fallen for her, Lilith, or the mortal vessel. The former reaction will get her blessing the other her curse but this is only my conjecture. In truth such encounters rarely kill the man but what of his soul? The text was written as a warning to men of the time to

keep away from the dangers of visiting prostitutes, the times were changing no more would sacred temple prostitution have any sort of respect in society as the old traditions were making way for the new. And to imbue the fear of a soul lost to heaven and committed to hell should he transgress the strict religious rules he was meant to adhere to sealed that fear in stone.

THE SACRED PROSTITUTES: LILITH / NAAMAH / EISHETH / AGRAT BAT MAHLAT

A definition of sacred prostitution in ancient Mesopotamia could be construed as a temple rite that involves sex. Whether a Goddess was invoked as part of this is debatable. There is some evidence that Temples to Ishtar and Inaana held such rites. So one presumes that a temple prostitute would be trained and employed to perform such acts. Goddesses strongly associated with sex, motherhood and fertility often had temple prostitutes. Having spirits/demons who are also seen as sacred prostitutes would seem to imply that the prostitute would be possessed by one of them during the rite, but this is speculation. To me their modern role seems a little clearer, they can be called upon to play a part in sacred sex or are met through spontaneous acts. There is also a tenuous link between an aspect now dropped from our own Maypole celebrations here in the UK and those of perhaps similar spring fertility rites in the ancient Near and Middle East. A 'bride' (usually a virgin) is chosen and deflowered in a ritual context by the local King/Lord etc to ensure good harvest. This tradition definitely existed here until the Middle Ages and there is some limited evidence that it also appeared in ancient Greece, Rome and Middle East. The sacred prostitute would be a virginal maid. If we take 'virginal' to imply not as yet had children or barren then Lilith and her sisters fulfil this role.

Naamah the demon, sister or daughter of Lilith is often argued

Naamah – Liliy Maid by Rupert Desnaux © 2018

to be the same as the Biblical Naamah, wife of Noah and sister of Tubal-Cain. The Kabbalah cites them as being the same being but many disagree and say they are entirely different. To overcome this and, perhaps, sate both sides it is possible to view Naamah the once mortal woman as dying and her spirit becomes the demonic one. Naamah is the name given to the daughter of Lamech, Noahs father, and Zillah his wife. Naamah is the twin sister of Tubal-Cain who is also accredited with teaching men metallurgy. I would dispute this as, if you follow the Biblical time line, when Naamah arrives bronze was already very established so it is most likely as an Iron worker he was best known. She is also cited as Noah's wife which might indicate that she is also Utnashiptum's consort also. She is meant to be very beautiful and accused of using her cymbals to lead men astray. Raphael Patai says in his book *The Hebrew Goddess* that she mated with an angel known as Shamdon and had Asmodeus by him. Asmodeus is also known as one of her consorts.

Naamah is often seen as more active in the succubus role than any of Lilith's counterparts.

Another quote from the Zohar says;

She makes sport with the sons of man, and conceives from them through their dreams, from the male desire, and she attaches herself to them. She takes the desire, and nothing more, and from that desire she conceives and brings forth all kinds of demons into the world. And those sons who she bares from men visit the women of humankind, who then conceive from them and give birth to spirits. And all of them go to Lilith and she brings them up...

This is very interesting, it seems here that only their desire for Naamah/Lilith is required to create demons. To me this makes sense. In purely energetic terms sexual lust is a powerful force and would be more than enough to create energetic forms from. 'The sons who she bares from men' are her demons/incubus then visit mortal women and conceive new spirits. There is a distinct difference here,

demons and spirits, demons being the thought form inspiration, energetic beings in their own rights but spirits indicates another level of existence, that are sent to Lilith who 'brings them up' raises them, we presume.

Rabbi Yitzhaq says of her . . . Those sons of God, Aza and Aza'el went astray after her.

The fallen angels are said to have bred with mortal women to create the giants or Nephilim. But here we have reference to two of the fallen being drawn to Naamah. The confusion between Naamah the lesser or younger Lilith and Naamah the possible mortal woman continues here. The conclusion being that they mated with her whilst she was in mortal form.

And Rabbi Shimeon said; She was the mother of the demons because she came from the side of Cain, and she, together with Lilith was appointed over the strangulation of children.

Naamah was a descendant of Cain and as such seen as inherently evil, her birth with her twin almost a direct physical reflection of their spiritual parents Lilith and Samael. She is also seen as one who would cause infanticide, specifically diphtheria.

This direct link back to the Garden proves that in Jewish beliefs the fact that Abel was pure and Cain tainted all goes back to Lilith and Samael taking Eve in the Garden of Eden. The belief from here on being that mankind was made impure because Samaels seed has polluted the earth and that his seed is responsible for all the evils upon the earth ever since.

We are given a picture of these two female forces working like a mother and daughter to bring up children between them, albeit evil demons.

And the quote continues . . .

At times it happens that Namaah goes forth into the world in order to have intercourse with the sons of man, and a man is found

in bounds of desire with her and is awaken form his sleep and gets hold of his wife and lies with her, and his urge stems from that desire which he felt in his dream. In such a case the child which is procreated comes from the side of Namaah, because in her desire was it conceived. When Lilith comes and sees this child, she knows what happened, and she attaches herself to him and rears him like the other children of Namaah and she comes to him many times but does not kill him. For each time when the moon renews itself in the world Lilith comes and visits all those whom she rears, and makes sport with them, and that man suffers damage at that time.

It is interesting that Naamah plants the sexual inspiration, as a succubus we presume, and yet once the children are recognised by Lilith as Naamah's she takes on the role of grandmother to them. 'She comes to him many times' but she does not kill them, she 'makes sport with them' and it causes the 'man' or father to suffer. The most likely reason she visits her grandchildren is to inspire them to do things that their father would disapprove of. And inciting rebellion is most definitely one of her strongest qualities. It is also thought that the 'sport' relates to sex and is another example of her succubus role. This is one of the clearest references I've found implying that 'Children of Lilith' are real. Lilith is barren, she is unable to have children of her own, she can influence their conception by sending Naamah, Samael, Cain etc. to men and women as they dream and fuel their desires but she cannot directly give birth to anything but demons. Those of us who believe we are her children know there is no doubt of it and she doesn't limit her offspring to boys, girls fare just as well as her kin. And we are certainly a global phenomenon. It allows us a direct line to her. It gives us access to her nature. This doesn't mean to say that a child of Lilith is limited to only working with her but she is likely to be the portal through which others can come. And just like any family there will be some they get on fine

with and others less so.

In other Kabbalistic writings Naamah is seen as the spiritual daughter of Qaftzefoni and Mehetabel and is the southern Lilith. The more traditional Lilith is still seen as the Northern Lilith and the elder version. This arrival in the Jewish peoples psyches of a grandmother and mother pair is not difficult to understand when you place the lesser or younger Lilith as Naamah. It also ties up with the normal mortal way of things where a young daughter replaces the mother for the sexual attentions of men whilst the older mother crones losing her fertility as her young daughter blossoms. And so the men that formerly sought the mother seek the daughter. But in her role of terrible mother she does not bare this advancement of age well and instead of accepting her maturity she fights against it and resents her daughter. And so this is taken out on the lesser Lilith who is scapegoated none the less. The elder northern Lilith is also held responsible for gynecological problems, infertility and all associated 'women's ills'.

Agrat bat Mahlat (Agrat daughter of Mahlat – mahlat meaning sickness in Hebrew)

This is another one given the title of Queen of Demons but is also described as being an angel. Female angels are rare, some say there are none. But I would argue that in some respects Angels are sexless. My feeling is that this one originated from Lilitu. She is of the air, and rides the sky, she dances on roofs whilst Lilith howls, specifically on Tuesday evenings and Saturdays. She is mentioned briefly in the Rabbinic texts of *Yalkut Hadash*. She is said to have a train of eighteen messengers of destruction. All these things have strong similarities with Lilitu. But this one is more sophisticated and is also held responsible for teaching a Jewish sage, Amemer, sorcery. She is known as the mother of Asmodeus and used King David as her inspired influence and seed. Only the spiritual actions of Rabbi Abaye and Hanina ben Dosa stopped her from having more power and influence over people.

EISHETH ZENUNIM

This one is thought to have been Samael's first wife and possibly the first documented succubus though many might disagree here and say that Ardat-lili can claim that title. She has qualities akin to Nemesis, and is a form of Ma-at or divine justice. Very little is actually written about her but she does turn up in Rabbinic literature. She is known as a fighter for women's rights and is the most warrior like of the sacred four but is rarely aggressive. Like Lilith she can both create and destroy life and has a lunar link. She usually shows up as a thin crone in gold clothing with six horns on her head which is also the number of horns on the Burney Relief and a number strongly associated with Lilith.

And so it transpires that the succubus developed a more sophisticated morphology. From being seen in her earliest days as Ardat-lili whom would prey on men whilst they slept to the young beauty Naamah and her associated family the succubus in this part of the journey became something less terrifying and more something understandable but to be protected against if possible. The reflective roles of sacred prostitute both spiritual and flesh is a fascinating subject. Those of the spirit are drawn to the flesh to inspire desire and lust and aid the creation of Lilith's children whilst those of the flesh are employed by temples/priests etc. to invoke spirits during sex and add a magical sexual dimension to their lives. So whether you are a child of Lilith, Samael, Cain or any other of this family you are born with their energy inside you. This affirmation of 'witch blood' being something some are born with and though not all recognise it or answer the call they have that added something extra whether they want it or not.

And that makes for just as much potential discomfort in today's world as it did when the Rabbi's wrote the Zohar.

THE TALMUD

Here she is mentioned again but only in passing. This doesn't mean to say she wasn't known to people at the time this was written in 400 CE quite the opposite, the relative ease at which her name is dropped implies she was well known and needed little explaining.

Shab. 151b footnote *"The night demon." "One may not sleep in a house alone, and whoever sleeps in a house alone is seized by Lilith."* This is normally meant as a warning to men rather than women and is often seen as a relating to her succubus role.

Rabbi Jeremia ben Eleazar said *"During those years (after their expulsion from the Garden), in which Adam, the first man, was separated from Eve, he became the father of ghouls and demons and lilin."* Rabbi Meir said, *"Adam, the first man, being very pious and finding that he had caused death to come into the world, sat fasting for 130 years, and separated himself from his wife for 130 years, and wore fig vines for 130 years. His fathering of evil spirits, referred to here, came as a result of wet dreams."* (Erubin 18b)

These comments are upholding the words of the Zohar but give a slightly differing view on Adams 'wilderness years'. Adam is often viewed as being full of guilt and a desire to do penance after the expulsion from the Garden. Lilith would have seen him wandering her domain as a gift and had great joy in using his sexual desires to create more demons from.

In Erubin 100b, footnote on a text describing Eve's ten curses regarding the eighth curse it is said, Eve is "*banished from the company of all men*"; In a Baraitha it is taught : "*A notorious female night demon." "She grows long hair like Lilith. Sits when making water like a beast and serves as a bolster for her husband.*" Eve is described as wearing her hair loose and free, this being not what a respectable Jewish woman would do. Orthodox Jewish women wear wigs and both early Christian women and most Muslim women

cover their heads. Both these Abrahamic paths see the need to lessen a woman's attractiveness to anyone except her husband. Only unmarried women are able to bare their hair in many branches of these religions. Hair is thought to have particular magical hold over men who are often attracted to women with long loose hair like Lilith. Prostitutes also have loose uncovered hair. This might also be where Lilith's promiscuous prostitute role originates. Some say she was Inaana's handmaiden and that Inaana was the Goddess of the women of the sacred prostitutes' temple in Sumer but this is also hotly debated.

Baba Bathra. 73a-b footnote to Hormin "a demon;" to Lilith "a female night demon".

"I saw how Hormin the son of Lilith was running on the parapet of the wall of Mahuza and a rider galloping below on horseback could not keep up with him. Once they saddled up for him two mules which stood on two bridges of the Rognag and he jumped from one to the other, backward and forward, holding in his hands two cups of wine, pouring alternately from one to the other and not a drop fell to the ground. Furthermore it was a stormy day such as that on which they that go down to the sea in ships mounted up to the Heavens; they went down to the deeps. When the government heard of this they put him to death."

Hormin is presumably one of Lilith's demon sons.

Rabbi Jose said, *"It once happened at Simoni that a woman aborted the likeness of Lilith, and when the case came up for a decision before the Sages they ruled that it was a child but that it also had wings...."* Nidda 166: v6, 24b footnote to Lilith *"A female demon of the night, reputed to have wings and a human face."* And regarding miscarriages, *"If an abortion had the likeness of Lilith its mother is unclean by reason of the birth, for it is a child, but it has wings."*

Birth deformities occur, often diseases can cause them and

hereditary factors, today we understand them better and rarely blame spiritual beings for their arrival but it seems Lilith was held responsible for such things when the Talmud was written.

Lilith makes a brief appearance below in *The Song of the Sage* from the Dead Sea Scrolls in Hymns against Demons.

4Q510 - Blessings to the King of Glory
Words of thanksgivings in psalms of
To the God of knowledge
To the resplendence of the powerful God of Gods
Lord of all the Holy ones
His realm above the powerful mighty
Before the might of his power
All are terrified
They scatter and flee from the radiance of his dwelling
Of his glory and majesty
And I the sage declare the grandeur of his radiance
In order to frighten and terrify
All the spirits of the ravishing angels
And the bastard sprits
Demons, Liliths, owls and jackals
And those who strike unexpectedly
To lead astray the spirit of knowledge
To make hearts forlorn
And in the era of the rule of wickedness
And in the periods of humiliation
Of the sons of light
In the guilty periods of those defiled by sins
Not for the everlasting destruction
But rather for an era of the humiliation of sin
Rejoice righteous ones in this God of wonders
My psalms are for the upright

May all of those of perfect path praise him.

This protective psalm or prayer is fairly common of those employed to give reassurance and spiritual insurance against those seen as a threat. Yet again Lilith is one held responsible for leading men astray, astray from Yahweh's laws and away from the moral indoctrination they are taught to follow as law. One has to be always aware she and her kind can strike at any time, constant vigilance must be held to protect one's own morality. Should they fall prey to her, guilt and humiliation will surely follow.

THE ALPHABET OF JESUS BEN SIRACH

But it is to the Alphabet of Jesus Ben Sirach that we find the most commonly known of and still to this day upheld image of Lilith as Adams first wife. This text was written at some point between 700-1,000 AD making it relatively modern by Lilith standards. And now it seems she has undergone a massive transformation. Most of the text is in the form of satirical proverbs and maybe that is how it should best be interpreted but it has carried much weight where the continual evolution of Lilith is concerned. It is said that King Nebuchadnezzar's son took ill and he called for Ben Sirach to heal him. Ben Sirach made an amulet and put the names of three angels on the reverse of it. Nebuchadnezzar wanted to know what these angels meant. And the translation of their conversation goes like this;

Said Nebuchadnezzar, *"Heal my son. If you don't, I will kill you."* Ben Sira immediately sat down and wrote an amulet with the Holy Name, and he inscribed on it the angels in charge of medicine by their names, forms, and images, and by their wings, hands, and feet. Nebuchadnezzar looked at the amulet. *"Who are these?"*

"The angels who are in charge of medicine who are, Senoy, Sansenoy and Semangelof. While God created Adam, who was

alone, He said, 'It is not good for man to be alone'. He also created a woman, from the earth, as He had created Adam himself, and called her Lilith. Adam and Lilith immediately began to fight. She said, 'I will not lie below,' and he said, 'I will not lie beneath you, but only on top. For you are fit only to be in the bottom position, while I am to be the superior one.' Lilith responded, 'We are equal to each other inasmuch as we were both created from the earth.' But they would not listen to one another. When Lilith saw this, she pronounced the Ineffable Name and flew away into the air. Adam stood in prayer before his Creator: 'Sovereign of the universe!' he said, 'the woman you gave me has run away.' At once, the Holy One, blessed be He, sent these three angels to bring her back.

"Said the Holy One to Adam, 'If she agrees to come back, what is made is good. If not, she must permit one hundred of her children to die every day.' The angels left God and pursued Lilith, whom they overtook in the midst of the sea, in the mighty waters wherein the Egyptians were destined to drown. They told her God's word, but she did not wish to return. The angels said, 'We shall drown you in the sea.'

'Leave me!' she said. 'I was created only to cause sickness to infants. If the infant is male, I have dominion over him for eight days after his birth, and if female, for twenty days.'

"When the angels heard Lilith's words, they insisted she go back. But she swore to them by the name of the living and eternal God: 'Whenever I see you or your names or your forms in an amulet, I will have no power over that infant.' She also agreed to have one hundred of her children die every day. Accordingly, every day one hundred demons perish, and for the same reason, we write the angels names on the amulets of young children. When Lilith sees their names, she remembers her oath, and the child recovers."

This is the story that gave us a whole new twist on Lilith. Here she seems to have demonic Lil-litu/Lili and Lamashtu qualities. But

never before has she been described as being created by Yahweh. It might well be that the baby killing Lilith had taken such a strong hold over the minds and psyches of the Jewish peoples that they had to give her some sort of myth and make sure it was all part of their ultimate creator Gods divine plan to include her. But why make her Adams first wife? The only answer possible is that by now she had already morphed into a powerful feminine force that represented the destructive or dark qualities of the divine feminine. In later Kabbalistic writings many methods for her creation are given, some saying she was made at the same time as Adam, some later and some before. But seeing as Genesis itself has two versions in chapter one and two describing mans creation that are in dispute with one another it is impossible to fully comprehend how the Jewish peoples saw Lilith's birth.

Regardless of the reason for the argument over sexual position between them the text implies that Lilith views herself as an equal to Adam and yet she can fly. This seems at odds with itself if you take into account beliefs at the time. She is called a demon by some and yet has wings, demons don't have them. Goddesses however do. Ninlil, Ishtar, Inaana and Lamashtu are all depicted with wings. Deities are also in many ancient myths form all over the world are sometimes alleged to be able to take physical form should they wish to, pure spirit doesn't. In Ben Sirachs text she knows Gods true name and uses it to make her escape. The fact that she, Lilith, is claimed to have known the secret name of God whereas his creation Adam didn't also implies a high status already existed for Lilith in the mindset of the people of the area at this time. She is caught up with in the Red Sea by the three angels who order her back or else one hundred of her children will die each day. What children? How can the first woman, apparently still a virgin by all accounts, have children? They meant her 'demon' children which places her back in demonic realms yet again. She then tells them to leave her be as she

was created to cause sickness to infants which puts her very much in the Goddess Lamashtu's territory again. And again makes no sense at all of why she, this alleged first woman, would be created to kill or injure infants when surely her mandate should be to have them? It is all very confusing. She finishes by giving them a get out clause and a way of protecting against her.

It seems to me that Ben Sirach needed a good tale for his King. And this was obviously something Nebuchadnezzar bought happily into. But it caught hold and grew wings of its own and by the time the Spanish were writing the Kabbalah it transformed yet again. But this is only my personal opinion and not the one upheld by the religious scholars of today.

THE INCANTATION BOWLS OF NIPPUR 600CE

So dangerous is she that Rabbis used to urge single men not to sleep alone in a house lest she come in and take their seed. Evidence of the extent of their fear can be found in the Aramaic Incantation bowls from Nippur. They were discovered between 1888-9 by Professor Peters of the University of Pennsylvania. Nippur was a Sumerian city originally and it's patron deity was Enlil. The bowls are thought to have been created between 500-600 BCE there seems too big a co-incidence for this their timing with the rise of the Babylonians and the eventual destruction of the Temple for it to be over looked. No where else so far has Lilith been mentioned quite so much in ancient history.

It also seems as though it is very important to actually know each demonic version of Lilith by name. Seen by the early Jews as representative of Lambartu or Lamashtu who herself has up to seven names, their fear of the demonic influence Liliths could inflict upon households was genuine and taken extremely seriously. Maybe this is because little evokes such fear as to lose a baby either before birth or soon after it. And yet prior to modern medicine and our

current ability to save many who would otherwise be taken from their families the high rate of such incidents was so common place as to increase their fears exponentially. In his book, *The Aramaic Incantation Bowls of Nippur James* by Alan Montgomery goes into great detail to understand and identify the sources and types of demons being exorcised or banished by the sorcerers who created the spells. And none feature quite so frequently as Liliths. On page 75 he says; *"But it is the Liliths which enjoy the greatest individual vogue in our demonology. Many of the charms culminate in that objective; the other evil spirits are most often merely generical, anonymous, to whom the general compliment of a spell must be paid, but the Liliths are definite terrors, whose malice is specific and whose traits and names are fully known".*

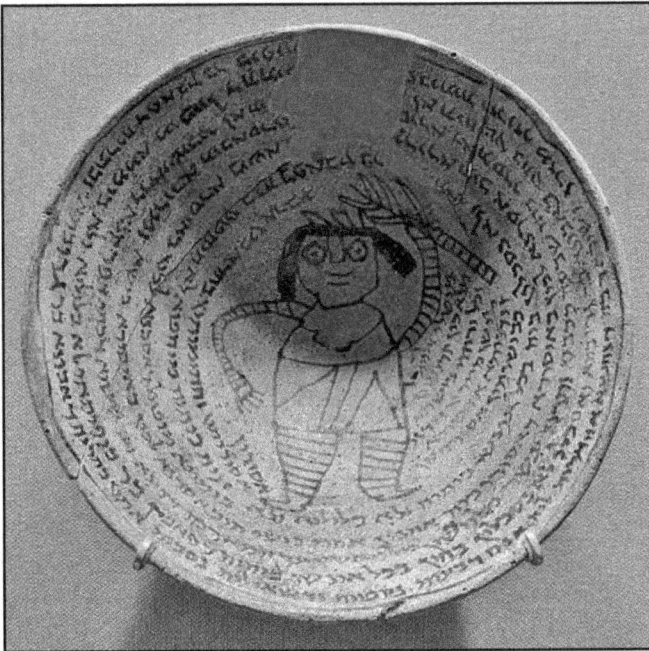

Over 40 bowls have been translated by James Alan Montgomery

and many include Lilith, Samael, Satan and even a few images of her. These simple clay bowls are inscribed with complex spells to protect people from many evils including Lilith. A common line found in many of them goes thus; *a ban-writ against all the demons and devils and Satans and Liliths and latbe.* This is found time and time again in many of the translated texts. Here we see the concept of multiple versions of Lilith and Satan in the minds of these Jewish peoples. It is as if they perceive their ability to attack many simultaneously meant they had to see them as many rather than embracing the concept that the one Lilith or Satan could actually be in many locations at once. Here we have one that is designed to protect a mother and child. *Health and arming and sealing and protection be for .... And the body and soul and the unborn child and womb of Bardesa whose mother is the daughter of Dade. Charmed are the sorcery spirits in stocks of iron; charmed are the Liliths in chains of lead; charmed the empoisoning male Devils and charmed the empoisoning female Liliths. Charmed the arts of evil men and hostile beasts and evil mysteries and the magic circle of malignant masters and sages and doctors and the melting of wax figures of him who is still alive from the unborn child and womb of Bardesa whose mother is Terme. Charmed the Lilith that appears to her in shape of Tata her sisters daughter; charmed all the defiling ghosts that have entered, which appear to her in dreams of night and in visions of day; charmed and sealed with the seal of King Solomon.*

In one such bowl Lilith is depicted as naked and wingless with long loose hair. Her ankles are chained and she has prominent breasts, and obvious genitals. This is the incantation on the bowl:

You are bound and sealed, all you demons and devils and Liliths, by that hard and strong, mighty and powerful bond with which are tied Sison and Sisin. . . . The evil Lilith, who causes the hearts of men to go astray and appears in the dream of the night and in the vision of the day, who burns and casts down with nightmare, attacks and

kills children, boys and girls -- she is conquered and sealed away from the house and from the threshold of Bahram-Gushnasp son of Ishtar-Nahid by the talisman of Metatron, the great prince who is called the Great Healer of Mercy . . . who vanquishes demons and devils, black arts and mighty spells and keeps them away from the house and threshold of Bahram-Gushnasp, the son of Ishtar-Nahid. Amen, Amen, Selah. Vanquished are the black arts and mighty spells, vanquished the bewitching women, they, their witchery and their spells, their curses and their invocations, and kept away from the four walls of the house of Bahram=Gushnasp, the son of Ishtar-Nahid. Vanquished and trampled down are the bewitching women, vanquished on earth and vanquished in heaven. Vanquished are the constellations and stars. Bound are the works of their hands. Amen, Amen, Selah.

Et occurent daemonia onocentauris et pilosus clamabit alter ad alterum ibi cubavit lamia et invenit sibi requiem

(And demons shall meet with monsters and one hairy one shall cry out to another, there the lamia has lain down and found rest for herself - 5 Vulgate)

LILITH AND THE SHEKINHA

Texts from the ancient port city of Ugarit in what is now northern Syria a Goddess known as 'Lady Athirat of the Sea' (Or she who treads upon or strides across the sea) is made mention of no less than twelve times in the *Epic of Ba-al.* Frequently mistaken for Ashtart or Ishtar who becomes Astarte and eventually the demon Astaroth, this creatrix Goddess is the wife of El and not, as in the case of Ashtart a daughter of El. Together Ba-al and Athirat have seventy children. She is also sometimes named as the female side of El. And so once again we have reference to a former androgyous deity splitting in two. Now biologically the female does come first

in human beings and so creates the male as Her companion. But ultimately we have the division of the sexes. She is a matriarch the first mother. She appears in Sumerian texts as a consort of Anu the sky God. In a place called Kuntillet Ajrud in the Sinai desert some storage jars were discovered dating back to the eighth century have inscriptions on them that pertain to Asherah and Yahweh with further detailing on invocations to these two in conjunction with El and Ba-al. That El, Ba-al and Yahweh are all one 'Lord' or derived from one another has always been speculated. Especially with there being described a Yahweh of Teman and another of Samaria. Now these could be separate Yahweh's (Lords) of each place and that would make sense. With Anu the Sky God being higher or more distant than the earthly 'Lords'.

Asherah as consort of each of these Lords and Queen of Heaven is also mentioned in the Book of Jeremiah, here there is mention of making prayers and offerings of cakes to her. She is also found in Hittite history as Asherdu or Ashertu. She seems to be a composite early creatrix Goddess whose influence traversed many cultures and belief systems even find herself re-incarnated in Egypt as Hathor. If Lilith is the dark side or hidden aspect of the earliest Goddesses of these parts then Asherah is surely her lighter more obvious half. This also makes sense where Yahweh taking her as his consort is concerned. She had feet placed firmly in the hearts and souls of Sumer and is generally highly thought of and loved in which ever guise or name she takes regardless of cultural beliefs.

This lady was held in high esteem by all cultures that venerated her. Many nude clay figurines thought to possibly be of Asherah have been found all over the Middle East especially around Palestine though these could belong to either Canaanite or Hebrew sources. But the more common ones believed to definitely be of Asherah were the Asherah poles. These little Goddess statues were made of wood and are described as 'planted' not placed in places people

wanted to associate with the Goddess.

It is generally believed that Asherah 'poles' were originally sacred trees and that the little carvings were most probably made from wood of these very trees so that people could have a little of their own Asherah planted in the ground near them.

She also found her way into the most famous Temple ever erected in this area, the Temple of Solomon had an Asherah statue in it for over 236 years of the 370 years it stood. She was the only Goddess to survive for so long in the hearts and minds of the Hebrew peoples and she only lost her ancient status with the invasion of the Babylonians and their destruction of the Temple.

Shekinha, she who is the divine feminine, and also more specifically the Shekhina, came to mean 'many' and was often cited as the 'dwelling place of God'. In this it is extremely tempting to say that only through communing with a female could you truly touch God. Through the acceptable face of femininity, Asherah the fertile mother Goddess of the Heavens, Yahweh became calmed and whole. She retains her status as first lady for some time. She is still at this point seen as the Queen of the Heavens. But this was not to last for very long. So Lilith is created first but seen as flawed and not suitable for either Yahweh or Adam but Asherah is. To an outsider this seems very simply selective. Early Hebrews were still polytheistic, monotheism comes quite some time later. So their God needed a consort, as all Gods do. It seems that Athirat/Asherah was chosen as the most acceptable one. She was a mother Goddess on a par with the highest of ancient Sumerian deities. And after the exile of the Jews both monotheism grows in popularity as does the migration of this Goddess to Jerusalem, temporarily. The God of the Canaanites that Abraham took his people to was El, not Yahweh. He was a mountain God and his consort was Asherah. They had a large family of seventy children the eldest and most prominent being Ba-al. To Jacobs's lineage Yahweh, one of the children or lesser Gods of

Ba-al and Asherah is appointed as supreme being.

So it might appear that Ba-al becomes Yahweh and Athirat becomes Asherah. Basically what we have here are imported deities. And as such they can be moulded to suit the new home they find themselves in. Lilitu/Lilith coming along for the ride with them. Her place being related but demoted to demonic realms. Where as elevating this God to monotheistic heights being just about as powerful as it gets. Not that this ever sat well then or now among many.

But who was Abrams (his name prior to migrating and receiving his call from 'God') original deity in Ur? It was most likely Naana, a Mood deitiy. He and his family were said to worship idols prior to his instructions to leave the area.

THE QUEEN OF SHEBA

Once tales of the legendary Queen of Sheba reached our shores so, possibly, did Lilith. She first pops up in Genesis 10.7 as a male with this name. There is also mention of one named Seba. But as The Queen of Sheba implies that Sheba is a place and not a name of a person it is confusing. Here she is Sheba, the son of Raamah who in turn is the son of Cush who is the son of Ham and son of Noah. In Genesis 10:26-29 there is mention of yet another Sheba whose lineage is traced as a descendant of Shem, another son of Noah. Geographically the first Sheba is from southern Arabia (Mesopotamia) and the other from Ethiopia. So it is possible that they are two separate individuals or could still be two and the same. Historical records not being entirely dependable at this time.

She was thought to have been born in the 10th century BCE and has many names. The Ethiopians knew her as Makeda or Maqueda, the Hebrews Malkat Sh'va, the Islamics called her Bilqis or Balqis. Whether she was a true ruling monarch is unsure and yet she seems to have had influence over a vast Empire. This encompassed parts

Makeba – Queen of Sheba by Gillian Macdonald

of East Africa, Arabia including the Persian Gulf and what was previously Sumer, up as far as Armenia and Syria. This certainly places her in Lilith's ancient territory.

She is best known for her legendary visit to King Solomon in Israel. She is drawn to him because she has heard of his high intelligence and ability to control demons or djinns. As I suggested above some say that Lilith and the Queen of Sheba were one and the same or that the Queen was half human and half demon. It is said that when she lifted her skirt her legs were excessively hairy from the waist down. Lilith is often called 'the hairy one' as mentioned in Biblical texts. She is also described as being an ultimate seductress and dancer. More qualities accredited to Lilith.

Sheba itself could well have been either a city or land as in a whole country. But there is no argument anywhere that it was a place. One possible location might have been a city known as Mareb in the Yemen as accounted in the Arabian world. Here one of her many names was Bilqays which is similar to some of the names given to her by the Muslim world. Makeba is the name the Ethiopians knew her as. And so it seems that the lady herself is known by many names, as is Lilith.

ETHIOPIAN VIEW

The Ethiopians record her as making a city called Azeba in their Book of Aksum but another book lists her as making Mount Makeba her capital city. Looking at historical records of Ethiopian lineage it is said that her mother was Queen Ismeni and that she was a part of a 350 year long dynasty that ended with Halle Sallesi in the 20th century. Ethiopian records vary and in some she is the daughter of King Agabo, possibly a descendant of the Agazyan tribe who also commanded both sides of the Red Sea at this time. This is the place cited as being where Lilith fled to after rejecting Adam. The King acquired his title after slaying a mythical serpent Arwe.

You certainly don't go very far when delving into Liliths mythology without meeting the serpent. In another version of this story it is Makeba herself who is threatened by the serpent or dragon as she has been left as an offering to it. As it is slain so some of its blood falls on her legs and turns them hairy, some also add that she gained cloven hooves. The obvious imagery of hairy legs and cloven hooves being linked in with wild beasts and pagan ways is also common to Lilith. Some say that she travelled to Solomon to be healed of this and it was his magical powers that drew her to him. So it is possible that the story that emerges much later in the Zohar of Lilith refusing Adam, going off to the Red Sea and then sending her consort or twin Samael/The Satan in serpent form to the Garden of Eden could, have originated from these sources among others besides including Sumerian legends.

The Ethiopian legends recorded in the Glory of Kings known as the Nebra Negast describes the history of Makeda. The most famous of all is the meeting with King Solomon. In this one she is said to have conceived Menelik who would become the first ever Emperor of Ethiopia. And it is he who would be entrusted with the Ark of the Covenant, the Ethiopians believing that it was a replica that stood in its place when the Babylonians sacked Jerusalem and that they have the original to this day. It is said that she heard tale of Solomon and his great wisdom and works and wished to visit him. She took him gifts of great value. For some reason best known to Makeda/ Queen of Sheba she asked the King not to try and take her virginity. This he promised as long she refrained from helping herself to anything in his palace. Now knowing Lilith's mythology as the first ever recorded woman to refuse a man and rebel against his wishes this would make sense. Solomon, being the cunning one he was, fed her lots of hot spicy food intended to make her thirsty knowing full well she'd forget her promise, or not care about it, when she woke dying of thirst a few hours later, which she did and

helped herself to some water. Solomon was waiting for this moment to strike and then she had to agree to sleep with him or else face a penalty for theft of such a valuable commodity as fresh water.

To taunt and tease a man is very Lilith, even by declaring a desire to remain chaste! And so Solomon might well have seen himself as the one who set the trap for the Queen but true to Lilith's style it was she.

But modern archaeologists place Sheba firmly in Southern Arabia which would discount the Ethiopian legend altogether!

HEBREW VIEW

The Hebrew references are quite different. There are no remarks of sexual intimacy between the two. That she visited him with an abundance of gold and jewels is mentioned in Kings 10:1-13. She is said to have asked him many tricky and clever questions. This is also very akin to Lilith's own nature. And when she wishes to impress a man she will go to any lengths. It sounds from Hebrew accounts that the two indulged in a mutual appreciation visit both being over generous with gifts for one another. And she left with them both being happy that a positive meeting of minds had occurred.

To believe that these two simply gifted each other with gold etc and had a cosy chat before she returned home apparently with no real benefit having been made seems unlikely. Travelling great distances in ancient times was dangerous and precarious. A great entourage of guards and horses would have been necessary. The route would have had to include safe watering holes and stop off points. This would have been a massive undertaking and a great risk especially if she was carrying such a rich hoard. To me it seems the Hebrew account is leaving something out. And that which is being left out could well be the mystical element of the meeting. Plus the possible romance between them.

THE ROMAN VIEW

The Roman writer and historian Flavius Josephus describes the Biblical Queen of Sheba as the Queen of both Egypt, Southern Arabia and Ethiopia. It is possible that she was a Queen but not a ruling monarch as those were usually men at this time in history. Flavius is keen on the Ethiopian location for Sheba and makes mention of a royal walled city named Saba in Ethiopia. At a later date this is also named Meroe which is also interestingly the word for merman or mermaid in Celtic. He describes it as an island with two rivers on either side near the Nile. This place is also thought to be linked with Moses.

THE CHRISTIAN VIEW

Here things take a strange turn. Here she is recorded as being the Queen of the South (Lilith is often called the Queen of the Southern Winds). Jesus mentions her as being one of the instrumental forces along with the Ninevites in judging those of his peers who reject him come Judgement Day. This is found in Matthew 12:42 and Luke 11:31. This seems a complete tangent to earlier records. To find her elevated to a judge of souls would imply she held a powerful and well respected spiritual position. It is said that the Magi who brought the gift of Frankincense came from the queens lands. That this resin is found in plentiful supply southern Arabia and North Africa there is no doubt. Emphasis is also placed upon her desire to retain her apparent chastity by getting Solomon to promise not to take her. Christian interpretation links this in with the Virgin Mary. She brought three specific types of gifts to Solomon, gold, incense and precious stones. This is also thought comparable to the gifts given to Jesus by the Magi as this passage from Isaiah quotes 60:6; *And they from Sheba shall come: they shall bring forth gold and incense; and they shall show forth the praises of the Lord.*

It is possible that during his 'lost' years Jesus travelled to the lands once ruled over by The Queen of Sheba's family and equally possible that he saw the Ark of the Covenant for himself. If the Ethiopian story has any grains of truth this would certainly help to explain partly why Jesus is said to have made this declaration. But modern scholarly thinking is that this is highly unlikely.

THE ISLAMIC VIEW

Here we find another tenuous Lilith link the Qur' an describes an instant where Solomon hears from a Hoopoe or hupula bird that in the land of Sheba the peoples worship a single Sun deity. Now this might have been spawned from the stories of the Egyptian Pharaoh Akhenaton's time. He invites her to his palace to turn her onto his God / Allah and instructs her to only worship this one true God. Not wishing a war with those she fears might enslave her peoples she decides to go and see him. Solomon summons a djinn to steal her throne and get it to him before she arrives and without her knowledge. Due to this act the Queen is so taken aback that he should have an identical throne to her that she converts to the Abrahamic path immediately.

MEDIEVAL VIEW

By medieval times she was inspiring great artists. She was also making appearances in some impressive locations including 12th century Cathedrals such as Chartres, Rochester and Amiens. In most cases it seems to be the moment of her offering gifts to Solomon that has been focused in on. In Strasburg Cathedral an image of her as the portal to the divine mother is depicted. This role of conduit to Asherah is often Lilith's hidden role.

And at a later date Boccaccio calls the Queen Nicaule, she who lived on a great island near the Nile (possibly Red Sea – Lilith's retreat) called Meroe as already mentioned above.

KING SOLOMON

That he was a wise King is well recorded and also responsible for building the first Temple at Jerusalem. He also created a series of channels and underground waterways to bring clean water into the city from a nearby spring. Evidence of this is there to this day. He was not only an architect he was also well versed in mystical knowledge in particular that of summoning demons or djinn to do his bidding. He and his craftsman King Hiram are held responsible for the eventual creation of the Knights Templar and stone masonry which in turn leads onto the birth of Freemasonry. All these elements pulled together helped to found much of the occult knowledge practised today.

The legendary Key of Solomon and Lesser Key of Solomon also known as the Book of Evil Spirits alleged to have been written in part by Solomon himself has, to some extent, survived to this day. In it are many angelic and demonic sigils and alleged incantations to summon djinn and demons. This book has led to many others exploring goetia magic including John Dee of Elizabethan times. This is not to be confused by the Book of Wisdom one of the many writings seen as apocryphal that was also written by Solomon. Three Books of the bible are ascribed to Solomon and they are The Book of Proverbs, Ecclesiastes and Song of Songs. The last is sometimes referred to as love poems inspired by the Queen of Sheba but Hebrews prefer to see this as a collection of verses in which a mere mortal man attempts to describe the love as between Yahweh and humankind.

Solomon's notoriety for being able to order demons and angels to do his bidding was legendary. It is said that he summoned such help in the building of the Temple at Jerusalem. Some might now suggest, me included, that ordering any spirit around is asking for a fall at some point and Solomon was not exempt. One such demon has been suggested as being Asmodeus. There are several differing stories

of power struggles between these two. Now here we have another link to Lilith. The younger Lilith also known as Naamah is said to be this demons consort. This Queen is the one who gave birth to his eventual main heir. Eventually Solomon falls from grace by taking many wives and indulging in idoltry. After such an illustrious career of temple and city building it seems surprising that such wisdom could fall foul of folly. And yet when we take into account the belief that Asmodeus as well as being King of Demons was also the Arch Angel and demon of lust it makes more sense. So perhaps Solomon was flawed after all. We all have our weaknesses.

SUMMARY

It is said she was born at some point in the 10th century BCE. But whether she originated from Ethiopia or Southern Arabia is not clear. There are enough folk tales and scriptural writings to prove that a Queen of status came from south of Israel and visited King Solomon for a specific purpose. That she was known as far south as Kenya is known for there the Luhya peoples know her as Nakuti. And as we know she was later known by the Romans and the historian Josephus Flavius as Nacaule. So her fame spread far and wide.

That she is known of, talked about, and remembered to this day, albeit shrouded in mystery, is very much akin to Lilith's own mythology. She is depicted as dark skinned with a powerful presence. Rich and resplendent in jewels. Lilith is also described this way in the Zohar.

So, the Ethiopians big her up and the Hebrews play her down. And if she was linked with Lilith this would also make much sense.

And if the Queen of Sheba was an incarnated Lilith she was not only Queen of Demons but also instrumental in the inspiration and creation of the Temple of Solomon. These possibilities were not necessarily known to our medieval ancestors who, if they had heard

of her at all, would no doubt have heard of the baby killing Jewish succubus rather than likening her to Sheba. But some modern day followers, myself included, believe that Ashmodai or Asmodeus was the main demon responsible for aiding in the creation of the Temple. Especially as he might well have objected to being bossed around by an arrogant King and planned to trip him up in his own way at a later date. Now whether this was inspired by Lilith the elder or younger isn't clear. If the elder one was partly a muse for it then she was also possibly instrumental in reacting to the fall of Asherah. This being the last Hebrew Goddess honoured at the Temple before its fall. And seeing as the temple would eventually house the Ark of the Covenant which in itself houses the Shekinah it would have been impossible for Lilith not to have been intimately involved with its conception and creation. Asherah was Yahweh's consort at the time of the building of the temple, he having taken her from her former husband El. She was mother to some 70 Gods including Baal. That she was the last remaining Goddess allowed a statue in the temple and that the Ark was a vessel through which she could join with Yahweh made her uniquely powerful and a last vestige of female divinity in Israel. To Lilith who escaped such control by being demonised and remains free to this day, the fall of Asherah was indicative of the patriarchal religious suppression of female divinity and rule that would come.

Another way of looking at the role of the Queen of Sheba is through Lilith's own eyes. To do this we have to imagine that Lilith is holding her reigns one way or another. No way would she be able to use her usual modus operandi on someone like Solomon. He was too astute and clever to fall for a nocturnal succubae. Nor could she simply inspire him directly, anyone who could trap and control her demons would smell a rat instantly. He worshipped Asherah so would be onto Lilith's energy as it tried to permeate through that door. No, she had to be as cunning as the one she wished to meet.

So she had to meet him on equal terms. This also appeals to Lilith. Going to see him as a rich Queen from another land baring great and wondrous gifts had a far better chance of working. Especially as she appealed to the male ego in wanting something from him that only he with his unique wisdom could provide. This was the lure she used on Solomon. And it worked. It is also entirely possible that she set out to deliberately cause the conception of a child by him. Much of this is hypothetical speculation but to me as one close to Lilith, it fits, perfectly.

In a purely simplistic modern view on the energies at work here we have, a time when the sexually independent wild and free spirited woman had already been demonised, aka Lilith and only the safe motherly one remained. And now even she was about to be rid of.

The birth of extreme sexism, divine female suppression and suppression of women generally was escalating.

The biggest irony being it isn't Yahweh Lilith had a problem with, she is risen to being his consort eventually by the Jewish peoples, its mankind.

CHAPTER THREE

THE GARDEN OF EDEN AND THE FALL FROM GRACE

No location in history has been debated and pontificated over more than this place, this alleged sacred birth place of humanity as mentioned in Genesis, the first book of the Old Testament. Was it born of the ancient tribal memories of a real place or a metaphor for a hidden wisdom, or both? Does it refer to a time period prior to the creation of cities and writing that people kept alive in traditional stories? Rabbis, theologians, scholars, anthropologists, and many more besides have dissected Genesis over the years and all have varying opinions and theories regarding it. The ideas and inspirations surrounding this first book of the Old Testament are often extreme. Lilith's role in this myth is twofold. Firstly she is written of in scriptures as Adams first wife in the Garden and that she refused to obey him caused her to fall from divine grace and secondly that she had a side role in 'the serpent's' temptation of Eve. So she is very much a part of this story.

It places Lilith at the heart of the Abrahamic creation myth. Thought to relate to around 6-7,000 BCE something we obviously now know not to be true. So what is this? To me it relates to a spiritual shift. Man will be as the Gods and know the difference between 'good' and 'evil'. Now this first book of the Bible does of course lay the foundation for all the laws, rules and guidance on what exactly constituted 'good' and 'evil' in Middle Eastern Jewish

Garden of Eden by John Collier

society over 6,500 years ago that follows in the subsequent books of the bible. And therefore as such isn't really applicable to anyone who chooses not to believe it or buy into it. And this seems to be why Lilith is here. It is as if she says, "There is another way, many ways, this isn't the only option, you can if you so wish, take responsibility for your own actions just be aware there are those who will chose to impose their rules and punishments for breaking said rules upon you" She is the obligatory challenge to the status quo. There is always one. But to follow her example puts you in danger of being an outcast and as such not offered the protection of living in a society. It presents a greater challenge, that of finding your own tribe. As she did. Among us, ironically. So the ultimate challenge of standing alone of being a self-reliant outcast from your culture does seem a part of her path and that of others among her kin. To me she also seems to be pointing out the obvious, none of it was perfect, that was the illusion. Once Adam and Eves eyes were opened they saw their nakedness and were shamed.

Hebrew Eden was not alone. Many religions and traditional paths have stories of Eden like places, the Sumerians being one such example. And as the Babylonians had a massive influence on the early Hebrew myths it isn't surprising to find strong parallels and similarities.

It is in the Apocrypha and the often seen as satirical Midrash, or meditation, known as the Alphabet of Ben Sira from the Wisdom of Jesus ben Sirach that Lilith makes an appearance in the legendary garden. And as the translation of the Latin Vulgate is disputed in its accuracy by many this did not find its way into the standardized examples of the medieval Bible or the King James Bible. But in reading through the first few chapters of Genesis, the first book of the Bible and Old Testament, the clues are there.

That Lilith/Samael both play important parts in this creation myth is disputed by some and upheld by others. My interest is finding

out what their possible hypothetical roles in this mythological place were. I am seeing it from a non-Judaic/Christian/Muslim perspective but I am buying into the concept that much human prehistory of the area history is weaved into their ancient texts.

This heavenly orchard was declared the first home of man in the Book of Genesis. The first concept to take on board is that they viewed it as a place of perfection. But the fact that this doesn't last and that some destructive presence enters it introducing disharmony is what makes it fascinating. And this aspect is also found elsewhere.

One is that this story might well have been *in part* borrowed from even older creation myths of other cultures and their religions in surrounding countries one example being, that of the Enuma Elish. This tale originated from Babylonia. Written in an ancient form of Akkadian it is agreed by many to be up to 3,000 yrs old. When placed alongside one another the openings are remarkably similar.

Both begin in darkness.

Light is then mentioned as being present before the creation of other heavenly bodies.

Both myths have the presence of matter prior to life being created. Both have the arrival of chaos from which order is achieved by a God.

The Sea Goddess Tiamat represents chaos in the Enuma Elish who is split in two by Marduk, this echoes the division of the waters above and below in Genesis.

The rest of the creations, animals and humankind etc. all follow in parallel suit.

The Sumerian paradise precedes the writing of Genesis and was known as 'The Garden of the Gods' here the high council of the Annanuki resided from on high. It was a garden in the mountains. In the Epic of Gilgamesh, the hero Gilgamesh visits the place known as

'Mashu' which is approached through a cedar forest. The so called 'Scorpion People' guarded the gates to the garden and the Sumerian for Mashu is 'twins' indicating the presence of two mountains in this heavenly place. Scholars Edward Lipinski and Peter Kyle Mc Carter have suggested that the location is between Mount Hermon and Mount Lebanon as the geography does fit the narrative. Mount Hermon also being a direct connection with the legendary fall of certain angels. The winged divine beings evident in ancient Mesopotamian, Assyrian and Persian art work are often thought to be the origins of the concept of angelic beings that evolved in the Hebrew beliefs. There is no doubt that the recording in writing of the Sumerian beliefs came first by virtue of the fact these people invented cuneiform text. And there is a pretty strong case for Lilith having originated from Sumer.

Many other important places mentioned in Sumerian texts refer to sacred gardens and both Nippur and Eridu are cities known for their temple gardens and sacred groves with 'trees of life'. Another famous one most people have heard of is the Hanging Gardens of Babylon. In the Eridu garden according to mythology only the Gods were permitted to enter the sacred gardens. A 'kiskanu tree' is watered by the Euphrates and the place is rich in Lapis Lazuli a semi-precious stone hugely revered by ancient peoples of this era.

And these creation myths and their hierarchy of Gods and Goddesses gave birth to demons and Liliths.

Scholars mainly agree today that Genesis was mostly put together in the 5th and 6th centuries BCE rather than being scribed directly by Moses. This places it in a time becoming all too co-incidental where Lilith's myth is concerned, it fits with the fall of the Temple and the invasion of Jerusalem by Babylonians. A time when the last revered Hebrew Goddess, Asherah, was also cast from said place. Asherah being a sea Goddess.

The Enuma Elish begins with a battle of the Gods and a division

that many liken to the falling out between Yahweh and Samael who is cast out and demoted to walk the Earth forever more as The Satan. And the Book of Enoch takes this further stating that a division of the angels occurred with some staying in Heaven and some following Satan. Here the legend of The Watchers or Grigori echoes the Sumerian myth.

So what we do have is a shift in thinking of the peoples of Israel compared to many of their polytheistic neighbours. Enuma Elish does indeed tell the tale of a divine war with one family winning over another and the descendants of that family reigning supreme as high council of gods immediately afterwards in the minds of the peoples at the time. Genesis also mentions 'Gods' plural due to polytheism still being the prominent belief system until quite some time later in our history.

The site of the garden has been hotly debated and has been identified as many varied places all over the world but Dr. Juris Zarin claims the garden is now very much under water at the top end of the Persian Gulf in Southern Iraq. It is described as being east of Israel at the convergence of four rivers. Two of these rivers are known to us as they still flow to this day and they are the Tigris and the Euphrates. The next river, the Pison is in the land of the Havilah which today is thought to be Wadi Riniah a place rich in bedellium, an aromatic gum resin, onyx and gold. It is especially interesting the book of Genesis takes time and trouble to describe this so carefully. The next, Gihon, Zarin says is the Karin river. By utilizing modern technology and using satellite images to see old river beds under the water he has almost conclusively proven this to be in alignment with the description in Genesis.

We now know that during the time of the supposed 'creation' peoples known as the Kushshites were living in this area but early Hebrews often passed through here and must have heard tales of the area. We know that the word Eden means bliss in Hebrew but it

is interesting to see what it means in ancient Sumerian considering the time period this myth is relating actually took place whilst Sumer was being created. The name Eden in Sumerian means 'fertile plain' and the name Adam means 'settlement on the plain'. These two pieces of illumination instantly click into logical place with the theory that these stories are old remnants of an actual historical truth even if most of it has been well and truly lost in translation. The flood related in the Bible and the previous Sumerian Epic of Gilgamesh could well have been a massive flooding in this area and with the rivers being so close to the head of the gulf any significant rise in sea water would lead to a massive tidal surge.

Zarin proposes that the act of disobedience wasn't anything to do with knowledge of good and or evil but instead the time in our history when humankind utilized their knowledge and tools to cultivate crops instead of merely trusting God to provide without intervention. To Zarin we suddenly went beyond the original vegan instructions in Genesis by herding and domesticating animals and sought to manipulate nature. And this could be true if the time scale fitted, which it doesn't. We know human beings have always been omnivores. humankind was farming before the alleged time of 'creation' as written about in the Old Testament. humankind was already settled and farming this area around 6,000 BCE. So this doesn't really hold up.

Most early Hebrew beliefs place the creation of the world by Yahweh being between 5,500 BCE and 4,000 BCE. Of course Darwinism, modern science and geology especially places the creation of our earth at around 4,500 Billion years ago. It is accepted by the vast majority of the world now that this is true.

The earliest evidence of farming permeating what is now Iran and Iraq came down with tribes such as the Hassuna, Samarran, Halaf and Ubadian. These were identified by their individual pottery styles and carbon dating. The Zagros Mountains is a place

thought to be where the first farmers originated but there are two migration theories that make the Samarra peoples different. This was about 8,000 BCE. The Kurgan pottery style came down from the Russian steppes and the Ukraine, these peoples were the first horseman and also had pottery and were originally nomadic.

The other migration theory is the Anatolian one that Lilith has inspired me to follow and investigate and came from an area that is now modern day turkey. The first of these peoples, the Hassuna, were thought to be around 6,000 BCE. They left evidence of pottery kilns, copper smelting kilns, bead work, the growing of barley among other cereal crops, and had got as far as domesticating, sheep, goats, pigs and cattle. This level of sophistication was entirely new to the area they moved into so it must have evolved from further north and possibly west.

Imagine what an amazing tribe these people could have formed once they met and traded skills, cultures and joined forces. This mega tribe of sophistication capable of farming with metal tools, herding animals on horseback, spinning yarns and making pottery would have been able to far exceed the existing abilities of other tribes. And their spiritual beliefs would have merged as well. Mixing the early Siberian and Ukrainian shamanic practices with the early ancestral and death traditions of Anatolia made for potent magic! And seems to have led onto the growth and evolution of religion in this area.

The Samarran peoples were seen as contemporary and at the same level of technological advances but had begun to irrigate water. But these peoples do interest us and differ in one major way from the Hussana, they left evidence of what might be signs of a goddess figuring in their beliefs. They made a large amount of clay female figurines and their pottery incorporated dancing girls. These peoples settled mostly in the middle of the Tigris and judging by the line of pottery excavated they must have traveled down from the

north, possibly from Ukraine.

The next people to settle the area with similar skills and knowledge were the Halaf. These people also left a snail trail of pottery from the North West. They are thought to be different from the former migratory tribes as their house style was unique and dome shaped rather than square. Their belief system included death rituals, burial rites and cremations. They also left female figurines that might be depicting a Goddess or several Goddesses.

The final contenders are the Ubadian peoples whose pottery style is recognized and whose skills are pretty much the same as the tribes preceding them over the last 1500 years. The Ubadian peoples settled in the area thought to be the second Eden and were most likely the peoples the second Genesis myth comes from. They have also left a trail from North West to south east in the area from Anatolia to the area that would become Sumer. These peoples were here from 5500 BCE. So it transpires that over a period of roughly one thousand years farming, metallurgy, water irrigation, jewellery making, gold and copper working, possible Goddess worship, and burial rites all made their presence felt in this area and it all seems to have flowed from the north east and north west of the area now known as Iraq. And so the first towns and cities were built with Jericho in the West and Eridu in the East being possibly the earliest.

Archaeological evidence for pottery, rudimentary copper work has been found that dates back to this period. They might well have been the first ever miners of ore. They brought their advanced knowledge with them. To the nomads of the wilderness these people must have seemed magical and supernatural in their mysterious abilities.

This amazing melting pot of cultures, ideas, skills all came together to create the first big cities. And it seems to have all occurred over several thousand years but does seem to have begun with the melting of the ice age. Rising sea waters and sudden glacial

ice floods would have pushed people south.

And with them on a spiritual level came shamanism, ancestral death worship/necromancy, Goddess's and Gods, paganism and witchcraft.

The signs and evidence at sites such as Gobekli Tepe and Catal Huyok all lead one to think these peoples had a ruling shamanic elite that were capable of organizing and motivating large numbers of people. It must have taken hundreds to create these earliest of temples. These pre-historic 'witchdoctors' were also thought responsible for teaching mankind many skills including herbalism and art. Art and sorcery came through an increased power to visualize.

But the most radical discovery of all is that it seems from the evidence being gathered that people began to settle at regular times in larger groups throughout the year because of their growing beliefs and a need to take part in rituals to mark them.

I'm not an anthropologist or an academic but it does seem to me that this massive turning point in spiritual evolution seems to indicate that the shamanic/animist path was changing. Why the priests of the time suddenly felt the need for a covered structure to work in is unclear. But what does seem evident is that they were now incorporating more people in their rituals. These rituals also seem to be more organized and last longer possibly involving many days and nights. And if you have many mouths to feed you might require more food than is locally readily available. If people gathered at this place for weeks at a time they might have herded animals and need to enclose them before killing them and eating them. This might well have been a sacrificial feast to mark a particular date or time. The suddenly elevated specialized skills of the early shepherds would most likely include ability to light a fire, protect self and herd from predators and stay vigilant. Learning some magical protection skills to add to your prowess was a good idea and so veneration

of the animals we relied upon at sacred times gave them sacred status in our minds. The shaman would travel, often thought to be in skin covered tents or in the case of Ukraine, yurts, inhaling hallucinogenic substances such as cannabis and other psychotropic plants and fungi.

Holy relevance of the shepherd cannot be underestimated in the case of the evolution of this area. What might have begun as a small seasonal side line in herding, taming and milking with specially trained people to do the work for group religious ceremonies grew into the massive food production industry we have today. And what started out as harvested wild einkorn or barley to deliberately planting the seeds and protecting the crops from other grazing animals also grew into the enormous wheat fields of the world today.

Before humans began settling for any significant lengths of time it is likely that dead relatives would have been left or buried and not necessarily returned to once this was done as life and the tribe literally moved on. The evidence uncovered at Gobekli Tepe regarding the peoples form of worship and type of ritual is not clear but the architecture they went to enormous lengths to build means this was a definitive time in spiritual growth. The doors to the temple rooms were round. This is important to note. The earliest temples might have been symbolic wombs for rituals of re-birth and possibly sexual ones also. And the temple room would have been dark except for oil lamps, a fire and incense. With the massive imposing ancestral stone monoliths looking down on you and the dancing flames causing shadows to dance around the carved animals it would have been like entering another dimension of being. It would have felt otherworldly. This place seems to incorporate both shamanic and new religious structure all rolled into one. As to what kind of rituals were held we can only guess but it is entirely possible that they served multiple purposes from seasonal festivals like the fruitful abundant time, to ancestral worship and death rites

of passage. The two largest central pillars were most probably to hold up a roof but might also have doubled as specific figures. My theory is that these two represent a mother and father of creation, the ultimate primordial parents. If one wants to view this from a Biblical perspective one could say that Adam and Eve were the first to build a temple in the new garden and that Cain and Namaah continued and developed all the skills and beliefs as a consequence of this.

The desire to settle came before the time of farming.

This is the opposite of previously thought history. From only recently emerging evidence we shall reveal how and why this happened and when you think about it you will realize just how simple it was. And with the side effects of this desire for a shared spiritual existence came greater and more complex religious beliefs. It is also possible for many new ideas, inspirations, art, new skills and tools and medicines to be born. Our original settled ancestors might have begun prolonged settlements for religious festivals and rituals but took to it in a much more serious way once smelting copper became a new past time. And with this came a massive revolution and the birth of another new concept, permanent towns leading to far greater cities.

And what exactly does all of this have to do with Lilith? My supposition derives from the fact that she led me to this line of thought for a reason. From death, her consort, came religious beliefs. Our collective reaction to death and our need to still maintain a link with our dead seems to have been the reason for the earliest religious and spiritual gatherings we have evidence of anywhere in the world. So in some respects a death cult gave birth to all the subsequent paths that followed, or so it would appear. Lilith as menstruation is death. Wasted life.

THE FLOODS AND THEIR PART TO PLAY

The first flood myth we have written evidence of from this part of the world is found in The Epic of Gilgamesh. This Sumerian account is thought to have occurred at some point between 2700BCe and 2500 BCE. The Biblical flood of Noah is thought to have taken place around 2348 BCE. With only a few hundred years difference between them they could be the same. It is entirely possible that many of the Sumerian legends and myths were based on real events and that Hebrews traveling through the land picked up on them.

Anu, Enlil, Ninurta, Ennugi, and Enki were the Sumerian Gods held responsible for the first flood but Enki was not that happy with the plan to wipe out masses of the people. He leaks the news. There are many who say Enki and Yahweh are one and the same. And there are those who say Enlil and Samael are the same. Enki lets a man known as Utnapishtim know of the planned deluge, just as with Noahs flood only Noah gets to know about it. Enki encourages Utnapishtim to use the materials his house is made of to build a boat in which to keep those he loves alive including animals. This also corresponds with the Biblical story. All of this takes place on the banks of the Euphrates in an area prone to seasonal flooding. Just like Noah's Ark this boat also has very specific dimensions given for its construction, very large dimensions are recorded. But Utnapishtim is worried about what others will say and so is told to tell people that he has fallen out with the God Enlil and decided to move to Enki territory. The territory he is to move to is believed to be Eridu. Much is made of the size of this boat, which just like the Biblical Ark is enormous. He loads it with food and water and living things and it takes a special launch way to help it into the water. A great storm now ensued. This storm is reputed to be so bad and so terrible that even the gods themselves 'cowered like dogs' from its force. The storm lasts for seven days. From accounts

of it many people were 'turned to clay' or drowned. Utnapishtim wept for the dead as his boat came to ground on mount Nimush. He then sets about releasing a dove that returns, a swallow which also returns and finally a raven which fails to return. This also has strong correlations to the Biblical flood story. After making several sacrifices to the Gods a Goddess arrives. The Goddess concerned is believed to be Ishtar. She says:

"Ye gods, as surely as I shall not forget this lapis lazuli [amulet] around my neck, I shall be mindful of these days and never forget them! The gods may come to the sacrificial offering. But Enlil may not come, because he brought about the flood and annihilated my people without considering the consequences."

Here we have an important falling out between a Goddess and a God which we liken to Lilith and Yahweh. And the fact that Ishtar saw them as '*her people*'. Or Lilitu's people perhaps? They might well be the same!

Enlil is reported to be furious that some people have survived. A general bickering and arguing commences between the deities who turn on Enki. Enki denies telling Utnapishtim and only admits to inspiring him in a dream.

This story is so close to the Biblical flood story of Noah's ark as to be identical. And these sorts of similarities between the myths and legends of ancient Sumer and later Hebrew texts cannot be over looked. Many have gone so far as to say that most of the stories of Genesis are indeed based on earlier cultures and their myths having been absorbed, re-told and utilised at later dates by scribes and priests wanting to have a creation myth of their own to project upon Yahweh.

There seem to be three important environmental catastrophes that affected the peoples of Anatolia and Mesopotamia from 10,000 BCE to 3,500 BCE and all might have been absorbed into stories handed down and eventually written in cuneiform.

The first is the retreat of the ice age and the movement of people away from the shores of The Black Sea.

I believe that surviving this catastrophe could have been what lead to the creation of Gobekli Tepe and the birthplace of all the future religions of the Middle East but this is my lay persons perspective.

The second flood myth is estimated to have been at some point between 2500 BCE and 2400 BCE this flood myth combines the one in The Epic of Gilgamesh and the Biblical one concerning Noah, both being seemingly identical. This one seems more of a freak storm that definitely affected the water levels of the tidal rivers.

The third one is Greek and concerns a great flood ordered by Zeus in around 1530 BCE and the hero of this very similar story is one named Deucalion.

It is entirely possible that more than one major flood story contributed to these myths. The oldest might have originated from Ice Age waters melting to volcanic eruptions such as Mount Ararat which is thought to have last been active around 3000BCE to heavy rains, so it is not surprising to find them here. Ironically the Biblical ark is meant to have come to rest on Mount Ararat. The boat constructed by Utnapishtim is meant to have come to rest on Mount Nimush. Again no archaeological evidence of this has been discovered. Ararat is in modern day Armenia but during Sumerian times was settled and called Ururat. If people fled to high ground to escape flood waters this area was a possibility. It is also linked with Abraham's family and his trip north. So there could even be a third regional catastrophe to have affected peoples of this area 3,000 years ago.

It is entirely possible, and highly likely, that the ancestral/ shamanic religion that emerged from Gobekli Tepe gave birth to our first ever named deities. It is also possible that a vague ancestral memory lay within the peoples of the fertile crescent of a garden, a

mystical paradise, a place from which life sprung and from where the earth was replenished. And until the earliest form of cuneiform writing emerged from Mesopotamia none of these memories would be recorded. We might never know the earliest ones but we do know many things. The majority of Genesis was written between 500-600BCE thousands of years after the alleged events it describes took place. The Kabbalah arrives even later in our consciousness. Many of these events might well link in with natural environmental occurrences and localized catastrophes. Many of these events are stories that were poached from Sumer and other cultures. Yahweh is not an ultimate creator deity he was a minor deity from Edom and Lilith might have evolved from Lilitu but then again she might not have.

Genesis One is to me a brave declaration of power that a nation was making by raising its God, Yahweh, to pole position in the heavens. At the time it was put together it was radical and very bold indeed. To be surrounded by polytheistic invaders and to claim spiritual superiority amid the chaos that was and still is fought to this day was awesome and incredible and proved if nothing else, Yahweh was a big player and main man and was here to stay, regardless.

But where Lilith is concerned Tiamat may well have been another of her counterparts. A Goddess of chaos and dragons and demons who is cast into the sea certainly sounds awfully familiar.

When examining the Biblical account of the creation of humankind I've tried to view it as partly historical. There is no doubt among historians that some chapters of the Old Testament or Torah do include much that can be directly related to actual historical events as confirmed by other texts from other neighbouring cultures of the time. And although modern science has proven the time periods for the creation of the earth and life on it to be in direct opposition of the alleged 6,000 yrs accredited to it in the Old Testiment the initial

gap in Genesis 1-1:2 is now frequently alleged to account for this apparent discrepancy.

I am only looking at Genesis for two reasons. One is that I have been directed here and re-directed here many times over the last few years by my muse and devotion, Lilith. And two is that according to the 8th to 10th century Alphabet of Jesus Ben Sirach, Lilith was Adam's first wife although it is never mentioned in most accepted forms of the Old Testament. I am looking to see if there might be a reason or a place for her in this scripture and what might have inspired Ben Sirach to include her in it. Naturally it could have been due to the need for a counter balance duality to Yahweh and Asherah by including Lilith in the creation myth with her male half Samael aka Satan. And I am also interested in what caused the myth of the Garden of Eden to be written about in the first place. And so it is to the first few chapters of Genesis that I first turned my attention.

As one of the most popular versions of the Bible in the West is the King James Version and that most subsequent re-writes have come from so it is this that has sufficed for this enquiry.

Apart from the seven day creation of the earth as we now know it there is a discrepancy between Genesis 1:26 and 2:7 both describing the creation of man but differently. This seems to be another gap. By now we are on the sixth 'day' of creation.

Taken from the King James Version:

1:26

And God said, Let us make man in our own image, after our likeness: and let them have dominion over the fish in the sea, and of the fowl of the air, and over the cattle, and over all the earth, and over every creeping thing that creepeth upon the earth.

(It is generally assumed the reference to 'us' and 'our' includes God plus angelic beings or Seraphim. But many people also presume

this to be in relation to multiple Gods existing in the mind sets of the peoples when this first book of the Bible was written. To me this embodies the time period prior to the arrival of writing after the retreat of the ice age. It allows for as long as tribal memories and oral traditional stories permit.)

1:27

So God created man in his own image, in the image of God created he him; male and female created he them.

(The assumption is that the reference to the 'image' of God infers less about the physical and more to do with the spiritual essence, but here it clearly states that both sexes seem to be created at the same time together. This essential difference is important. It seems to imply that men and women were viewed as spiritually equal prior to the need for a second creation of man.)

1:28

And God blessed them, and God said unto them, Be fruitful and multiply, and replenish the earth, and subdue it: and have dominion over the fish in the sea, and over the fowl of the air, and over every living thing that moveth upon the earth.

(This seems to imply that mankind had already existed prior to this apparent initial creation and that numbers were so low that they needed replenishing. This would fit the post-catastrophe or near extinction theory)

1:29

And God said behold I have given you every herb bearing seed, which is upon the face of all the earth. And every tree which is in the fruit of the tree yielding seed; to you it shall be for meat.

(This appears to view early mankind as vegetarian which we know from archaeological finds in the area wasn't true.)

1:30

And to every beast of the earth, and to every fowl of the air, and to everything that creepeth upon the earth, wherein there is life, I have given every green herb for meat, and it was so.

(This implies that the other life forms were all taken care of where their nourishment was concerned)

So, to summarise, we have man and woman created at the same time to replenish low human stocks and given all they need to survive on. This very statement is at odds with itself. How can one have the supposed initial creation of mankind at a time when it also declares that mankind already exists? Only if a new type of human being was to replace the previous variety. And we know that physically we were exactly the same 6,000yrs ago as we are now. So if it is to make any sense it must include a massive change in the way people of the area were to view themselves from this point onward. To me this seems the most honest description of a time when mankind was in danger of extinction.

Then we move forward to Genesis 2 and things take a weird turn.

2:7

And the Lord God formed man of the dust of the ground, and breathed life into his nostrils, and man became a living soul.

(The second creation of mankind as told in Genesis has only one man created and as yet no woman. The emphasis here seems to be establishing a patriarchal order. The previously 'soulless man' is now given one. This appears to reflect major religious changes occurring within the Hebrew society at the time of this being written down.)

The Alphabet of Ben Sirach in the 8th century claims that Lilith was Adams first wife. This seems omitted from most versions of the Old Testament. To keep this book very much on the Lilith current it is important to decide when she arrives. If she is a creatrix Goddess

then she was most definitely around way before mankind. The Apocyrphal writings of Enoch 1 were written prior to the bulk of the Old Testament and might have been accessed by Ben Sirach and helped to inspire his work. Some of these texts were also found in the Dead Sea Scrolls and verified the age of the work.

The first creation of humankind included women and was merely that. No individual names are given or gardens are mentioned. It is indeed obvious that something profound in the thinking and beliefs of the time changed dramatically or else why have this detailed description of the second creation. It seems the first creation were left to get on with their apparent lifestyle of equality and be happy. So what went wrong?

If the women plural in the first creation myth were all 'Liliths' then it would explain why she was given to Adam as a wife. She was already there, a wild and free human being and equal to men. Eve however most definitely isn't. She is created from one of Adam's ribs.

2:21
And the Lord God caused a deep sleep to fall upon Adam, and he slept: and he took one of his ribs, and closed up the flesh instead thereof;

2:22
And the rib which the Lord God had taken from the man, made he a woman, because she was taken out of man.

2:23
And Adam said "this is now bone of my bones, and flesh of my flesh, she shall be called woman because she was taken out of man.

This second creation of man seems to be saying that woman is only of a man and not an entire equal. She was created from him. And yet this is in conflict with the knowledge that it is women who

bare children. It would be easy to view this as a need to have the original creation deemed the reverse so as to make sure we know that man as in the male sex came spiritually and religiously first with women a very clear second. It is also easy to view this as a need to raise the profile of men to a higher nature than women and create the gender bias that has ruled the bulk of the Abrahamic paths ever since. But it might also be due to the fact that at this time in our collective past we didn't know anything much about females having eggs inside them. It was generally thought that the female was the receptive vessel or grail for the man to fertilise. The semen was seen as the only seed required. But it doesn't explain why Genesis states that they were created equally the first time. And with the next two verses describing the marriage a man will make with his woman it also must have some bearing on the sanctity of relationships between the heterosexual couple. It seems they learn about the two becoming one flesh and are enlightened to the divine pleasure of sacred sexual union. This 'marriage' is now being declared as the ideal, the acknowledged and the preferred by God.

2:8

And the Lord God planted a garden eastward in Eden; and there he put the man who he had formed.

(As covered earlier the word Eden has two possible origins, one is the Akkadian and Sumerian word for 'plain or steppe' but more recently it is thought to have derived from the Aramaic word for 'fruitful or well-watered' which seems more likely. In Hebrew Eden means bliss or pleasure. The Sumerians also have a place called Dilmun which was the dwelling place of the immortals where sickness and death were unheard of.)

2:9

And out of the ground made the Lord God grow every tree that is pleasant to the sight, and good for food: the tree of life also in the

midst of the garden and the tree of knowledge of good and evil.

(Now we have direct reference to these mythical trees, the trees whose arrival in our consciousness gave rise to the Kabbalah. It is important to note here that many ancient religious cultures have a Tree of Life or sacred tree, this concept seems rife in our collective spiritual growth. The Scandinavian culture has Yggdrasil, The World tree, Druids venerated Oaks, Vodhun has the tradition of planting a sacred tree in each new village community, and other examples are too numerous to list.)

2:10
And a river went out of Eden to water the garden; and from thence it parted, and became into four heads.

2:11
The name of the first is Pison: that is it which compasseth the whole land of Havilah, where there is gold;

2:12
And the gold of that land is good: there is bdellium and onyx stone.

2:13
And the name of the second river is Gihon: the same that compasseth the whole land of Ethiopia

2:14
And the name of the third river is Hikkekel : that is it which goes towards the east of Assyria . And the fourth river is Euphrates.

2:10 - 2:14 Seem to give Eden hunters geographical references from which to identify the location of the legendary place. That it is

described linked with rivers here on this plane of existence seems to imply Eden was less a heavenly abode separate from Earth but very much a part of it. It might well have been an especially beautiful place. It could also have been a lush and green place of fruits and rivers and abundances of plants and animals not to mention trees. It almost sounds like an oasis.

So for those who ascribe Eden to being a metaphor for a time of paradise it probably was but it does seem a localised one and not the possible reference to a time prior to the tilt of the earth causing the arrival of seasons. Those who buy into it being a reference to the vertical poles theory may find this specific location somewhat defies this premise. Plus why go to such lengths to describe fairly accurately where this garden was if its location was not meant to be identified. It would have been just as easy, if not more so, to invent names of mythical rivers.

Two significant locations are given for Eden, if it actually existed. One is near Lake Van in what was Anatolia and is now modern day eastern Turkey and the other is Dr. Zarins' hypothesis that it is at the head of the Persian Gulf. The origin of the Euphrates, one of the four rivers cited as springing fourth from one river, is indeed in the Turkish mountains. But that the river rises does not necessarily mean that it is its source. It can also imply that it is on higher ground than the land around it meaning either location can be relevant. Jerusalem is also proposed but lacks many of the geographical landmarks.

My own view is a challenge to these two and I propose that *the entire Fertile Crescent is a Garden of Eden.* And my reasoning is thus.

Firstly it is important to gain a picture of the time scale involved here and look for signs of the earliest religious evidence in this area. For that see south eastern Turkey and an area that includes places such as Gobekli Tepe, Catal Hoyuk, and Catal Neroli. And

further down in to the west we have Jericho possibly the oldest city discovered so far.

There were constant migratory paths from Anatolia down to what is now modern day Israel, Lebanon and Jordan and following the Euphrates down to modern day Iraq. There were also migratory paths from Ukraine and Northern Iran down to Iraq. And from the Far East also.

Most of the surrounding land around the Fertile Crescent is deserts and mountains. Once agriculture and settled permanence took hold so claiming parcels of fertile land also occurred and the most surprising theory of all is that it was a change in spiritual beliefs that altered our previously nomadic existence.

But all this came many thousands of years before the writing of Genesis and it is unlikely that an accurate oral tradition might have kept any story intact for such a long period before scribes were able to commit it to stone or parchment.

THE FALL FROM GRACE

There were two significant falls that Lilith played a part in. One is the fall of her consort Samael to earth with many of his kind in rebellion of Yahweh and the other is the fall of Adam and Eve and the ejection from paradise.

Firstly we will look at the Angelic descent.

Man fell from the perfect paradise of the Garden of Eden through temptation, or so Genesis tells us. But Lilith and others had already fallen from divine grace way earlier. The most popular apocryphal scripture concerning the fall of certain angels is *The Book of Enoch*. Here we find the leader of the Watchers or Grigori a particular group of Angels falls out of favour with God due to finding the children of God sexually attractive. The result of this fall being the creation of the Nephilim. Semjazza is accredited with

leading this rebellion but it is not long before Azazel replaces him and appears to be given higher status and greater supernatural qualities. It is popular today to view Azazel as the offspring of Lilith and Semjazza. Now considering Lilith can only bring demons into existence it would follow that Azazel would be viewed as one. And yet he is often cited as being the first born Nephilim. Traditionally Nephilim are a combination of angels and mortal women, giants. So how can Azazel fall into this category? He doesn't. He seems created to lead the Nephilim in their cause to wipe out the little faces or children of God and replace them with these giant hybrids. He is different, unique, and held responsible for all the sins of mankind. The ceremony of Atonement or Yom Kippur would send a live goat out into the wilderness, Lilith's repose, with all the sins of man placed upon its back. The offering of this live goat to Azazel spares mankind from God's wrath in punishing sins for another year. The ceremony is complex. It also involves burnt offerings and libations of blood placed upon the four corners of the Ark of the Covenant as is set out here.

Azazel in the Old Testament of the Jewish Bible or Tanakh in the book of Leviticus as written by Moses. Here are these words from Leviticus for you to find him in.

6: *And Aaron shall present the bullock of the sin-offering, which is for himself, and make atonement for himself, and for his house.*

7: *And he shall take the two goats, and set them before the LORD at the door of the tent of meeting.*

8: *And Aaron shall cast lots upon the two goats: one lot for the LORD, and the other lot for Azazel.*

9: *And Aaron shall present the goat upon which the lot fell for the LORD, and offer him for a sin-offering.*

10: *But the goat, on which the lot fell for Azazel, shall be set alive before the LORD, to make atonement over him, to send him away*

for Azazel into the wilderness.

11: And Aaron shall present the bullock of the sin-offering, which is for himself, and shall make atonement for himself, and for his house, and shall kill the bullock of the sin-offering which is for himself.

12: And he shall take a censer full of coals of fire from off the altar before the LORD, and his hands full of sweet incense beaten small, and bring it within the veil.

13: And he shall put the incense upon the fire before the LORD, that the cloud of the incense may cover the ark-cover that is upon the testimony, that he die not.

14: And he shall take of the blood of the bullock, and sprinkle it with his finger upon the ark-cover on the east; and before the ark-cover shall he sprinkle of the blood with his finger seven times.

15: Then shall he kill the goat of the sin-offering, that is for the people, and bring his blood within the veil, and do with his blood as he did with the blood of the bullock, and sprinkle it upon the ark-cover, and before the ark-cover.

16: And he shall make atonement for the holy place, because of the uncleannesses of the children of Israel, and because of their transgressions, even all their sins; and so shall he do for the tent of meeting, that dwelleth with them in the midst of their uncleannesses.

17: And there shall be no man in the tent of meeting when he goeth in to make atonement in the holy place, until he come out, and have made atonement for himself, and for his household, and for all the assembly of Israel.

18: And he shall go out unto the altar that is before the LORD, and make atonement for it; and shall take of the blood of the bullock, and of the blood of the goat, and put it upon the horns of the altar round about.

19: And he shall sprinkle of the blood upon it with his finger seven times, and cleanse it, and hallow it from the uncleannesses of

the children of Israel.

20: And when he hath made an end of atoning for the holy place, and the tent of meeting, and the altar, he shall present the live goat.

21: And Aaron shall lay both his hands upon the head of the live goat, and confess over him all the iniquities of the children of Israel, and all their transgressions, even all their sins; and he shall put them upon the head of the goat, and shall send him away by the hand of an appointed man into the wilderness.

22: And the goat shall bear upon him all their iniquities unto a land which is cut off; and he shall let go the goat in the wilderness.

23: And Aaron shall come into the tent of meeting, and shall put off the linen garments, which he put on when he went into the holy place, and shall leave them there.

24: And he shall bathe his flesh in water in a holy place and put on his other vestments, and come forth, and offer his burnt-offering and the burnt-offering of the people, and make atonement for himself and for the people.

25: And the fat of the sin-offering shall he make smoke upon the altar.

26: And he that letteth go the goat for _Azazel_ shall wash his clothes, and bathe his flesh in water, and afterward he may come into the camp.

27: And the bullock of the sin-offering, and the goat of the sin-offering, whose blood was brought in to make atonement in the holy place, shall be carried forth without the camp; and they shall burn in the fire their skins, and their flesh, and their dung.

28: And he that burneth them shall wash his clothes, and bathe his flesh in water, and afterward he may come into the camp.

29: And it shall be a statute for ever unto you: in the seventh month, on the tenth day of the month, ye shall afflict your souls, and shall do no manner of work, the home-born, or the stranger that sojourneth among you.

For Azazel'. Azazel was obviously known to Moses and his people. And yet very little is written about him in a Biblical sense. No explanation is given as to who Azazel is and it isn't until the *Book of Enoch* that we hear more of him.

This son of Lilith is accredited with teaching mankind metallurgy, specifically the art of forging weapons of warfare. He also teaches women the art of cosmetics so increasing their attractiveness to their fellow men and in so doing increasing their lusts and lowering their restraint, this leading to adultery. The result of all this activity is the flood, deliberately caused by Yahweh to destroy the Nephilim with only Noah and his family spared.

Now I am not saying that this is in anyway historical as such, but it does always help to have a scapegoat to cast blame upon for wars, loss of morals, rebellion against ethical boundaries and all perceived evil and sin in the world. There was a need at the time of 1 Enoch to explain all these things. This apocryphal work written so it is believed at around the first century BCE is older than the New Testament and yet bares some similarity in context at times. It is not accepted scripture today apart from in Ethiopia. To find any written accounts of his fall we turn to the *Book of Enoch*. Here we have the story of his fall from grace. In 2.8 we read;

"*And Azazel taught men to make swords and knives and shields and breastplates; and made known to them the metals [of the earth] and the art of working them; and bracelets and ornaments; and the use of antimony and the beautifying of the eyelids; and all kinds of costly stones and all colouring tinctures. And there arose much godlessness, and they committed fornication, and they were led astray and became corrupt in all their ways.*"

And so Yahweh is said to have sent Raphael to cast him into a pit in the desert in a place named a Dudael, and bind him from encouraging any more sinful behaviour.

Further on in Enoch 2:8, Yahweh says, "*On the day of the great*

judgement he shall be cast into the fire. The whole earth has been corrupted through the works that were taught by Azazel: to him ascribe all sin."

Anyone who works with Lilith will, at some point encounter Azazel. His energy is intense, he is her lust in masculine form, his name itself when translated from Hebrew means 'strong of God' and it is often implied that he is on a par with Yahweh. He is born of the Black Sun, an eclipse. He also seems to come at night. His birth was said to make the sun burn brighter. To me his people are the Bedouin, the desert people. Goat herders. Their ancestors might well have been the first to discover metal. He, and his fallen cohorts were bound in 'Hell' or cast down unable to ever reach their previous celestial heights. They, like the serpent, are to crawl upon the earth until the day of Judgement when they, including Lilith will be destroyed. Allegedly.

But it seems that to ensure the survival of the Nephilim post flood, Lilith ensured Naamah mated with Noah to corrupt his pure seed and in so doing created the lineage many are familiar with in Tubal - Cain. This grandson of Azazel seems to have inherited the family tradition of metal working and made sure Lilith's spirit continued for as long as we survive.

Azazel is often called Satan and even Lucifer but to me these are three separate beings. Satan had a respectable and acceptable position as tempter and accuser of humankind. He was there to test our moral integrity and resolve to adhere to religious doctrine. The strong influence of Zoroastrianism in the Middle East offered an alternative title as Devil and adversary in Angra Mainyu who might well have played a part in his evolution. Most agree that the Samael of the Talmud is both the Arch Angel of Death but also the Satan and patron of Edom. He is also a consort of Lilith. Samael rules the seventh heaven and is the serpent in the Garden of Eden. Together with Lilith they created Asmodai or Asmodeus the 'Sword

of Samael' who becomes the King of Demons. He is also known as the blind god.

Lucifer the Morning Star or Venus is an entirely different angelic energy and yet they are frequently labeled as being the same. Lucifer was originally seen as the bringer of dawn, the light, the illuminated one. With origins that might well have developed from the mythologies of Ishtar and Inaana the descent from heaven is disputed heavily among scholars. Some saying it was more to do with the fall of the Canaanite God Attar and his descent into the underworld. There are many roots to the one we now know as Lucifer and it would fill a chapter all on its own to relate all of them and nowhere but from King James onward does the name become linked with Satan. Lucifer's light is in some respects fixed, anchored down here on earth balanced out each dawn and sunset by the appearance of Venus. Some who work with Lilith also combine Lucifer's energy finding that the two balance one another out and some see them as consorts, father daughter and even siblings. There does seem to be a strong attraction for one another so it is also unsurprising to find if you are connected with Lilith then Lucifer might also turn up at some point. To me Lucifer is ancient and wise bringing a gravity to ritual helping to earth and yet remain celestially connected.

All the fallen angels seem to have an affinity with Lilith. She almost seems like the one stirring the celestial pot. The fallen matriarch, she who opposes any form of order placed upon her and prefers to create and destroy her own. These days only three angels are acknowledged and accepted by the current Catholic faith, Michael, Gabriel and Uriel. Although Raphael is often tolerated. And yet the modern fixation for angels is huge. And thanks to people such as Doreen Virtue there seem hundreds for people to chose from, should you wish to. I have no idea where she found them all! But, the fallen, those among us, are not accepted. They are still cast as Devils there to cause evil and strife in our lives. The good/

evil monochrome spiritual world of this 'New Age' is not new. It is old and worn. To me the fallen allow us to make our own mistakes, encourage us to question laws, authority, and stretch our moral boundaries beyond cultural and religious dogma and indoctrination. They are the real liberators.

According to the *Book of Enoch* it is to the gap in the creation myth in Genesis that the fall of the angels occurred. This so called 'gap' has spawned a multitude of theories. One popular one is that the fall of the angels led by Semyazza accounts for the division.

The book itself is separated into two *Enochs*, known as the *Ethiopian Enoch* and *The Secrets of Enoch* which is the Apocalyptic text. It is not arranged in chronological order as the first few chapters are actually the youngest with the first five chapters being the newest. There are four books within the book. '*The Apocalypse of Weeks*' which is the oldest pre-Maccabaean part. '*The Fragments of the Book of Noah*' which is also pre-Maccabaean; '*The Dream Visions*' written about 165-161 BCE; '*The Book of the Heavenly Luminaries*' 110BCE; '*The Parables*' or '*Similitudes*' 105-64 BCE.

And although this book had always been included in the Ethiopian Church it has been left out of the Biblical texts. And even when in 1947 remnants of the same text as in the Ethiopian book were found in the Dead Sea Scrolls it is still not accepted as being genuinely written by Enoch prior to the flood.

It is in *Enoch 1*, 6.1 that we find reference to the fall.

And it came to pass, when the sons of men had increased, that in those days there were born to them fair and beautiful daughters. And the Angels, the sons of Heaven, saw them and desired them. And they said to one another: "Come, let us choose for ourselves wives, from the children of men, and let us beget, for ourselves, children." And Semyaza, who was their leader, said to them: "I fear that you may not wish this deed to be done and that I alone will pay for this

great sin." And they all answered him, and said: "Let us all swear an oath, and bind one-another with curses, so not to alter this plan, but to carry out this plan effectively." Then they all swore together and all bound one another with curses to it. And they were, in all, two hundred and they came down on Ardis, which is the summit of Mount Hermon. And they called the mountain Hermon because on it they swore and bound one another with curses. And these are the names of their leaders: Semyaza, who was their leader, Urakiba, Ramiel, Kokabiel, Tamiel, Ramiel, Daniel, Ezeqiel, Baraqiel, Asael, Armaros, Batriel, Ananel, Zaqiel, Samsiel, Satael, Turiel, Yomiel, Araziel. These are the leaders of the two hundred Angels and of all the others with them.

To explain how beings occupying another dimension appear here on this earthly plane almost sends us into the realms of science fiction and yet to cross dimensions might well be exactly what we all do constantly without truly ever realising. My own feeling is that they found a way of physically manifesting on this plane of existence and were able to leave the inner planes but that is open to much debate. (Explaining the Luminaries, Sun, Moon, Venus and their transit in orbit also accounts for the alleged fall, hence the reference to the Morning Star in the Bible Isaiah 14:12 *"How you have fallen from heaven, morning star, son of the dawn! You have been cast down to the earth, you who once laid low the nations! You said in your heart, 'I will ascend to the heavens; I will raise my throne above the stars of God; I will sit enthroned on the mount of assembly, on the utmost heights of Mount Zaphon. I will ascend above the tops of the clouds; I will make myself like the Most High.' But you are brought down to the realm of the dead, to the depths of the pit. Those who see you stare at you, they ponder your fate: 'Is this the man who shook the earth and made kingdoms tremble, the man who made the world a wilderness, who overthrew its cities and*

would not let his captives go home?" The confusion between the identity of Lucifer or Venus and Satan or Samael is often thought due to *Dante's Inferno* and John Milton's *Paradise Lost.* The verse itself has more to do with the fall of a Babylonian King than the luminary.

If Venus is Lucifer and the Moon is Lilith then the Sun would represent Yahweh. But naturally like all of these things it is up to individual belief, interpretation, inspiration and understanding and open to conjecture. But it does make for a Heavenly family with her spiritual 'child' Azazel being born of the black sun. Returning to the fall of the Angelic ones in *Enoch 1,* 7.1 it is even more interesting for here they are credited with teaching people herb craft and magical enchantments. This could be construed as healing.

By *Enoch 1,* 8.1 we have the arrival of Azazel who teaches people metallurgy and cosmetics. Eventually all the fallen inspire all manner of things including, medicine, science, astrology, writing and mathematics. But the two most offensive and sinful teachings seem to be metallurgy and fornication. For although sex was very much a part of life they are thought to be the ones who inspired mankind to enjoy it to all extremes, and so all forms of sexual expression not condoned by the religious paths of the day were sinful ones.

In the Qur'an the angels do not have free will and cannot sin because they were not granted the freedom by God to disobey which would mean the djinn Iblis cannot be a former Angel in their beliefs. When God created Adam, he ordered all the angels and Iblis to bow down to Adam as was termed "the Best of Creation". All the angels did so. The djinn Iblis refused to obey, and was brought into a state of rebellion against God. For this God cast him out of the Garden, and intended to punish him. Iblis begged God to delay the punishment until the Last Day (the Day of Judgment): this God granted, as he is Most Merciful.

It is We Who created you and gave you shape; then We bade

the angels prostrate to Adam, and they prostrate; not so Iblis; He refused to be of those who prostrate.

God said: "What prevented thee from prostrating when I commanded thee?" He said: "I am better than he: Thou didst create me from fire, and him from clay."

Qur'an, Sura 7, Ayat 11-12

Iblis was proud and arrogant and considered himself superior to Adam, since Adam was made from clay and Iblis from smokeless fire. For this act of disobedience, God cursed him to Hell for eternity, but gave him respite until the Day of Judgment, after Iblis requested it. Iblis obtained permission from God and vowed that he would use this time to lead all men and women astray to Hell as a way of revenge against them. By refusing to obey God's order he was thrown out of Paradise and thereafter he was called "Shaitan."

He said: "Give me respite till the day they are raised up."

(Allah) said: "Be thou among those who have respite."

He said: "Because thou hast thrown me out of the way, lo! I will lie in wait for them on thy straight way:

"Then will I assault them from before them and behind them, from their right and their left: Nor wilt thou find, in most of them, gratitude (for thy mercies)."

(Allah) said: "Get out from this, disgraced and expelled. If any of them follow thee,- Hell will I fill with you all.

Qur'an, Sura 7, Ayat 14-18

Although God allows the request, he also warns Iblis that he would have no authority over his sincere 'ubd "devoted servants".

"As for My servants, no authority shalt thou have over them:" Enough is thy Lord for a Disposer of affairs.

Qur'an - Sura 17, Ayah 65

And by the 8th to 10th centuries the Zohar was being written and we have the arrival of Lilith although many would say she has been here all along.

There is a reason for this. Rabbinic scripts of the Talmudic period tell us of a missing story that didn't make it into this instantly confusing introduction to the Bible. Lilith isn't mentioned by name and neither is Adam in the first creation myth. And once she does arrive in texts there are up to five different versions to contend with. Some say Lilith created herself as a pure soul that rose up out of the abyss or void. Some say she is a great dragon born on the fifth day when 'God' created the living creature in the waters which gives us the tenuous link with Leviathan although he is described as most definitely male we have to remember that Lilith is also described as androgynous. And then that she was created equally from dust with the first man. Or that she was created before Adam from unclean dirt and filth making the female instantly labeled with negative connotations. And the last is that they were originally androgynous but sawn in two so creating a separate male and female half.

But that it was felt necessary to include Lilith in the first creation story seems an attempt by the writers of the Talmud to come up with some sort of socially acceptable explanation for the two creation stories of man. By inserting Lilith in the first instance they can suddenly come up with a very good reason to create Eve the compliant obedient wife for Adam.

In some ways this dichotomy is quite simple, it marks the time that the roles of women were being redefined to suit the religious and political peoples in power when these scriptures were being re-written. Your choice as a woman was simple, marry who ever your family choose for you or risk being seen as troublesome and a potential problem to your family and society. As we return to the Garden and the first man and woman we can see why. Lilith not only refuses to obey Adam as a consequence of his forceful attempts to dominate her she runs off to the Red Sea to lead an unbridled promiscuous life.

So Lilith's behavior explains those troublesome women. She

represents the minority of girls who disobey their fathers and prefer an independent life. The irony being that any women who failed to secure husbands or refuse to accept one often found themselves having to do things such as prostitution to survive. For those women who chose the sisterhood over the duty and responsibility of marriage and raising children, sex for money was an alternative. And if the girl was pretty enough she would usually earn a reasonable amount. To generalize the reasons women found themselves as prostitutes during the 8th - 10th centuries could be seen as erroneous but refusing to marry is one such example. And then there were those who preferred to be the paid mistress, the sacred prostitute, she who only served a select few rich clients and had a marriage of sorts but not one that intended bearing children. Any women who rebelled against the social norms of the time were seen as potential Liliths. This especially applied to those who chose a sexually liberated life style taking multiple partners. And even being naturally barren was seen as a sign of Lilith's involvement and meant the girl concerned was cursed from birth or that her family were being punished.

Unimpressed with her rebellious behavior 'the lord' sends three Angels, Senoy, Sensanoy and Semangelof to order her return. She refuses to and is said to give 'God' a message, "*Let me be, for I was created in order to weaken the babes; if it is male I have power over him from his birth until the eighth day of his life, (Jewish boys are circumcised on the 9th day which is believed, among other things, to protect them from Lilith) and if born a girl then unto the twentieth day*". Now the Angels asked her not to do this and she replies, "*Whenever I shall see your names or images on an amulet, I shall do no harm to the child*", she agreed to allowing 'God' to destroy up to 100 of her demonic brood per day. Lilith takes further delight in deliberately visiting Adam by night in her succubus role and creates more of her demonic children by him.

And so Lilith is now a Goddess whose soul came out of the abyss and whose birth was from the waters. But was she also re-created in mortal form? If she fell from grace her punishment might well be to be cast as a mere mortal. And the fact that one of the births tells of 'God' making her from the dirt and filth it also fits into a creature who is flawed or diseased or, in the case of Genesis, less than her perfect male side kick Adam. She refuses to obey Adam; this is the crux in her story. This act of disobedience is not appreciated, this woman is not to be ordered or coerced into obliging anyone because this lady is fiercely independent and dominant. She is the one who came first after all so it could be construed that she wanted dominance over Adam. Here we have a direct link between the philosophy of the time that women should obey their husbands (Something that still to this day is enforced in some religious paths and societies) and that they should be submissive. Lilith is not submissive, she doesn't have a submissive bone in her body, Lilith is very much the archetype for the modern day dominatrix.

The argument over which sexual position to take is the crux of this matter. In some instances it is said that Adam wants to take Lilith in the missionary position but Lilith refuses him. In others it is said he tries to mount her as if a beast of the fields. She does not see why she should succumb to a man made of clay. We are not told what it is she wants and whether it is simply a matter of who goes on top. But this one small example of male domination as actually written down in ancient religious texts of the Middle East does seem to have helped spawn the feminist movement in other parts of the world in more recent times.

And if you view this as a Goddess about to have sex with a mortal it is likely the Goddess would take the upper hand, so to speak. If you view it that the feminine divinity has to be connected to Adam before he can access his inner divinity it also makes sense that Lilith might want top position. Going on top makes it easier for

the woman to control the experience and Lilith is rather fond of sex so might well want to adopt what becomes her traditional position. Plus divinity at the time was always viewed as being 'on high' as in above in a literal sense.

As it is she doesn't get the chance to and so she utters the secret name of 'God' which she mysteriously seems to know, and flies off. Here we have three noteworthy points to examine. One, that rape back in these ancient times was not a crime and that any man had the legal right to take his wife by force if he so wished. Two, that she knew this so called 'secret name of God', how she, the first woman, knew this is never explained unless of course she wasn't a woman in the first place. And, three, that she flies off, so this proves she has wings, which mortal women are not normally known for and nor are demons. These three discrepancies or revelations whichever way you wish to view them stand out as massive indicators of Lilith's true status. If she was viewed by religious peoples of the time as a divine Goddess they wouldn't expect her to submit to a mere mortal man. As a Goddess she might well know 'God's true name and be prepared to use it which she did. And finally as a Goddess she could well have the ability to fly as they are frequently depicted with wings, demons however don't have them, angels do. And so she escapes from Adam whom she clearly isn't impressed with to the Red Sea which the Hebrews of the time viewed as a place rich with lavacious demons.

Other accounts or versions of this same story claim Lilith flew to the desert to escape Adam. Either way she fled. And now that she has done so she sets about creating demons.

To me all this really means is that Lilith is the part of any woman who takes flight from any situation she doesn't like or feels threatened by. She is a woman with a back up plan and a desire to be herself regardless of the consequences.

It seems that to Ben Sira she is a Goddess on a par with Yahweh

who is claiming to be the one and only ultimate deity. This would make her the one and only Goddess if Asherah didn't already exist as his initial consort. Yahweh offers her his first man. The only reason this could be true is if Lilith represents the Holy Spirit and he is hoping she will be prepared to share some of her energy and imbue men with divinity. And this in itself is held up by many on an Occult path today.

This marker is very important for it informs us that God alone cannot create divinity and for divinity to be present here on this plane the female or Goddess energy is required. Now if we accept that even the biblical account itself gives away the fact that other people did exist at this point and that the world simply required 'replenishing' then this so called first man was simply the first of this particular 'God's people. In asking a Goddess , in this case Lilith, to aid him in creating a new race of divine men and women he was supporting the hypothesis that these new people would be elevated from the rest. The fact that his creation, Adam, seems to have had all the tact and diplomacy of a rhino at full charge meant the plan failed. But did it?

The concept of 'inner divinity' is at the heart of most Mystery Schools and Kabbalistic teachings. The belief in this was also taught by Jesus of Nazerath. It can be found in Sufi wisdom, the teachings of the Essenes, Hindu and Buddhist teachings. Not to mention the rising wave of New Agers. And yet to claim a direct connection and inner harmony with your divinity seems to cause unrest to many paths and traditions. To seek to find the inner divinity can seem arrogant or egotistical and yet those are two qualities most teachings advise you learn to surrender if you wish to connect comfortably. To imply that one person can by training reach this state of being does not go down well with many of the established Churches and Mosques of the world. As men and women we are to look up to our heavenly family and see ourselves as sheep.

This is not Lilith's path and so much of the wisdom remained secret or occluded. It was practiced by the few and they risked persecution and even death to reveal their knowledge. Free thinkers have always threatened the established order. And in this I see Lilith as another Hekate, a Queen of Witches. Witches live on the edge of society. They always seem to refuse to totally conform. A part of each witch is always in a state of rebellion against constructs that seek to bind and blind people. They occupy liminal spaces and work with liminal spirits. They frequently work with the ancestors and have communions with ghosts. This places them apart from others. And most of all above all else they are labeled as witches by their society once they curse successfully. A witch has his or her own morals not ones forced upon them. A witch takes responsibility for themselves.

But getting back to the Garden of Eden, Lilith has flown, Adam is alone and still needs a mate or as described in the Biblical texts, a 'helpmate'. So God puts him to sleep and removes a rib to create Eve. Eve is the opposite of Lilith. She is willing and submissive and compliant. She is a mere mortal and therefore cannot give man soul only God can hope to do this now. But this is an unbalanced soul it is only half a soul it lacks the divine feminine. He still has to breathe the Holy Spirit into man. One presumes in this case it is Asherah, the Matronit.

It is also interesting to note that the Sumerian for healing is 'ti' which also means rib in Hebrew. This might be pure co-incidence but it seems to have a link. By taking a rib from Adam to create Eve Yahweh is in effect attempting to heal the wound that Lilith is held responsible for making.

THE APPLE MOMENT

It is hard to avoid seeing a greater or hidden message in this text. Adam and Eve are given precise instructions not to eat from

the tree in the centre of the garden. Many older traditions than the Judaic have sacred trees whose fruit must not be touched by the communities that revere them. This superstition might well have found itself into the mind sets and beliefs of the time that Genesis was written.

Chapter 3 :

Verse 1 - Now the serpent was more subtle than any beast of the field which the Lord God had made. And he said unto the woman 'Yea hath God said, Ye shall not eat of every tree of the garden?'

Verse 2 - And the woman said unto the serpent, 'We may eat of the fruit of the trees of the garden'

Verse 3 - But the fruit of the tree that is in the midst of the garden, God hath said 'Ye shall not eat of it, neither shall ye touch it lest ye die'

Verse 4 - And the serpent said unto the woman, 'Ye shall not surely die: 5- For god doth know that in the day ye eat thereof then your eyes shall be opened and ye shall be as Gods.'

Verse 6 - And when the woman saw that the fruit was good for food, and that it was pleasant to the eyes, and a tree to be desired to make one wise, she took of the fruit there of, and did eat. And gave also unto her husband with her and he did eat.

Verse 7- And the eyes of both of them were opened and they knew they were naked; and they sewed fig leaves together and made themselves aprons.

It is said that if he does eat of this tree he will know the difference between good and evil and be as the Gods. This seems to imply man went from an intuitive instinctive path to a morally imposing one. There is a sense that we should all know the difference but morality is fraught with grey areas and only kindness and humanity can ever hope to aspire to such ideals. Even then the animal kingdom and nature itself might well have opposing views. Nature does

not recognize good or evil. There is no such thing. There is simply nature. It is also mentioned that at the time of Adam and Eve before the fall they were naked and not ashamed. This seems to be saying to me that they were instinctive and natural and then changed to take on guilt and self-consciousness.

But it is not Adam who first tastes of the fruit, it is Eve. By placing the female in the role of first disobedience we are echoing Lilith. She has already disobeyed. Now Eve follows suit. And it is the serpent who is the cause of this. Serpents are given a male prefix in Hebrew and so the assumption that the serpent was male is generally upheld. But there are many on the Lilith current today who prefer to see the serpent as a manifestation of Lilith. Traditionally going by the oldest texts found it has always been seen as male. The serpent is seen as being more subtle. More subtle than what is not explained. It is often seen as cunning or more intelligent.

The 'serpent' is accused of encouraging Eve, the woman, to eat of the forbidden the fruit by saying, "*Yea hath God said ye shall not eat of every tree in the garden?*" But as we can see he merely inquires as to her awareness of the rule thus far. She acknowledges this fact by directing the serpent to the tree that is forbidden. The serpent, knowing better than Eve, informs her that the fruit will not kill her either to touch or to eat. It is the serpent that lures her by informing her that the fruit will give her divine insight. And it is also possible that the tree and its fruit are a metaphor for something different. Up until now Adam and Eve have not copulated, or so it seems to imply, sex might well be the lesson the serpent is giving Eve. Why else would they suddenly be ashamed of their nakedness? Because their God will be able to pick up on their sexual activities that is why.

Many on the Lilith current also see this as the moment that Lilith and Samael use Eve to seep their own seed and energy into her. Her first sexual act with Adam produces Cain, Cain is the one who goes

onto kill his brother and is outcast as a consequence. Cain is often seen as a child of Lilith and Samael albeit a magical one. And that is, in my eyes at least, what constitutes a witch, one born of a magical union that includes participation of extra divine interventions. Merlin is one such example from British Legends. It is no surprise that Cain is so popular among modern day witches and occultists.

Straight after being ejected from the Garden of Eden Eve and the serpent are cursed. Adam is not. Eve is told all women will bare terrible pains during labour because of her actions for ever more and the serpent is told he will have to slither along on the ground and risk being trodden on. They are both punished and demoted. Adam is also demoted for doing what Eve told him to do. The Tree of Life that might have granted Adam and Eve immortality is suddenly placed under guard by cherubim as mankind falls to earth. Now there are labour pains, death, disease and hardships to deal with. This might well be merely the scribes using the creation of mankind as an opportunity to further demonize women and now cast blame for all sin at their doors. Plus in the Kabbalistic teachings that sprung from these mysteries the female force is seen as negative and the male as positive.

Soul will inspire ego and self to find its greatest happiness through what is best for its development and growth. This isn't the simplistic 'good' and 'evil' that many perceive it to be. One person's good being another's evil etc. hence the beguiling of Eve by the serpent. Soul could be viewed as parasitic it resides in the flesh of man and transcends the physical plane after death and is eternal. Samael knew that the fruit, or magical sexual union, with Eve would release her from the limitations of the earthly domain and liberate her. This liberation being the sacred sexual Holy Communion with divinity or 'God' through the powers of death as delivered to her by the serpent. And we have to bare in mind the serpent was still seen as a tool of 'God'. Samael also wanted Eve to enjoy sex to revel in

lust and abandonment.

The sexual sin of the Garden of Eden is written into the medieval Kabbalah and various Jewish Midrashes during the 9th century. Rabbi Max Eichhorn inspired by this went onto write "Cain: Son of the Serpent" at this time The Gospel of Philip cites the apple moment was purely sexual and the deliberate creation of Cain but is rejected by Protestant Churches as heresy. The Midrashes also claim that Cain was created minus a soul and that two beings had sex with Eve as in this quote from the Zohar:

"Two beings [Adam and Nachash] had intercourse with Eve, and she conceived from both and bore two children. Each followed one of the male parents, and their spirits parted, one to this side and one to the other, and similarly their characters. On the side of Cain are all the haunts of the evil species; from the side of Abel comes a more merciful class, yet not wholly beneficial ~ good wine mixed with bad." (Zohar 136)

It is also written in later rabbinic texts and that Adam was punished for having sex with Eve during her period. By bringing this into religious dogma then new rules concerning menstruation can be endorsed.

And so Eve sat under the tree in the garden with the lion headed serpent who watched as she partook of the fruit. Eve did not, it seem, care at this point whether she lived or died. It would also imply that death was as yet a mystery to this Eve. Here is born the ability in humans to disobey parental advice, an act nearly all of us indulge in at some point in our lives. The fact being that disobedience is often fun and though the lessons can often be harsh they are learned none the less. And as each delicious morsel melted in her mouth so she tasted life, not death, and she knew this proved she, Eve, could transcend death. But what part of her did this?

If, as Lilith has taught us, we view the serpent that Samael rides as Lilith the mother of life or the kundalini energy that links us

all to the divine then this would seem to imply that humankind, prior to this act of disobedience, was merely instinctive just as animals seem to be. He goes from merely fucking to learning of a far greater pleasure, a divine one. And here is where things take a most peculiar turn, after their fall from grace they suddenly they see their nakedness and are ashamed and cover their sexual organs with fig leaves. This perplexing reaction to discovering the knowledge of good and evil is the underpinning of the true knowledge. For why would you on discovering this monumental sudden awareness see your naked body as suddenly evil? Many place sex as the original sin. And the fact that a massive sexual revolution was about to occur makes some sense of it. And yet if you place sacred sex into the equation and Eve falling from grace by copulating with Samael it paints a clearer picture. Serpents have varying mystical and spiritual interpretations depending on the tradition you follow. But in this case the open or none esoteric aspect of the knowledge is that the serpent depicted intelligence or cunning. The apple moment has another mystery hidden deep within it. The Zohar also cites Samael as injecting his 'filth' into Eve and he is the one held responsible for fathering Cain.

The hidden or occult knowledge is that the serpent also meant our own spines and our ability to grow closer to the creation energy of the universe or 'God' by loving union through either sacred sex or other means. In disobeying God Eve was taking a step beyond the mandate, she was tempting her own fate and so we all do every time that we go against the wishes of others for our own benefit. By not obeying blindly we took our fall, we found the void, we were transported into a level of awareness that meant we had to take responsibility for ourselves. We also tapped into our own divinity and it terrified us.

Kabbalists see this fall as the part of human nature that gives into temptations it knows it shouldn't. They uphold the notion that the ego led Eve into straying and that we have all had death, Samael,

and suffering to deal with ever since and that true happiness or Edenic bliss can only be found through rising above our weaknesses and temptations in life. They are less inclined to view Eve as a sign that all women are inherently evil these days preferring to liken her to an inner Eve we all possess. To me this still seems twisted somehow. Through Lilith we see it slightly differently. Samael, the Angel of Death visits us, all of us eventually. And as orgasm is sometimes described as 'the little death' to have the act of creation, sex, at the centre of this myth does seem relevant.

The tree is the open secret. The fruit could be both a literal fruit and a symbolic one. The Kabbalists say there were three important trees in the Garden of Eden, the tree of life, of knowledge and of death. To this day people will tell you it was an apple tree in the centre of the garden but I am not convinced. The clues are, that the trees grew in Lebanon, have a link with the subject matters they represent and the characters portrayed. Lilith's tree is the willow, she is the one linked with death and Asrael or Samael, the willow is an eternal immortal tree. The tree of life was most probably either the date palm or the olive it is a tree whose fruit is the most generous in its life giving properties and life enhancing ones also but eating of these literal fruits does not give immortality. The tree of knowledge and love that they were banned from eating was almost certainly the pomegranate. It is prolific to the area that was once thought to be Eden. It also grows in Lebanon. It is linked with love/sex through being an aphrodisiac, hence probably why Aphrodite was linked with them and also has moderate contraceptive qualities. Making it an all round useful fruit should you wish people to avoid knowledge of such things. The hidden aspect of the fruit is the sex Eve indulged in with Samael. The very word pomegranate comes from the Latin pomum meaning apple and granatus, meaning seeded. So we have the source of the apple association.

The feast of Sukkot is celebrated by the Jewish peoples and is a very old festival that may well go back to pre-biblical times. It lasts

seven days and is to mark the fruit harvest. There are four trees that are seen as spiritually significant here and they are the willow, date palm, myrtle and citron. This feast would be most inspiring to the early scribes that wrote the first scriptures. This feast of fruit, fruit in its literal sense and can also include all the harvest of the year and any mortal fruit born. This might also be a remnant to the Eden moment. The garden was obviously in fruit when Adam and Eve fell from grace. But seeing as whether fruit was cultivated in a garden, or not, it still fruits at the same time. The possibility of humans celebrating abundant times is extremely likely and harvest celebrations probably one of our most ancient annual traditions.

It would appear to be that the arrival of organised religions in this area were due to several major reasons, firstly changes in lifestyles and technologies moving from hunting and gathering to farming and metal working, and secondly the emergence and success of death cults, shamanism and the concept of divinities. Death played a much closer part of our lives in these times. Indeed it is only up until relatively recently in our modern history that child mortality has been reduced dramatically and the population has exploded as a consequence. If you only expected one in five children to survive to adult hood then you lived with death, much death. In fact the majority of death our ancestors experienced was infant death.

In the beginning was the word and the word was God. Our need for language and communication came a long time into our human evolution but to assume it was due to spiritual awareness or divinity is unlikely. The inspiration for these new beliefs was death, death of those we love; death in large numbers, and death needing explaining and being seen as sacrifice. Gobekli Tepe might well be the birthplace of religion but it was a religion born of death and sacrifice as all the off shoots of these early temples would soon prove. All the Abrahamic religions were born of blood sacrifice and if you count circumcision, then the Hebrew path still does practice this sacrifice.

CHAPTER FOUR

LILITH
FROM MEDIEVAL TO PRESENT DAY

MEDIEVAL HEBREW LILITH

Many will say her roots are found hidden in the Jewish Kabbalah and therefore most probably originated from the 12th century. The Judaic Mysticism found in the texts of the Zohar probably originated from an earlier date and was most probably written between the period of 539BCE and 70CE. It reached Spain by the 13th century and became more widely known throughout Western Europe at around this period in history. And it most definitely mentions Lilith as we already know. Here she is viewed by the men of the time as the evil side of the divine female or embodying the true,'Nature of Nature' as in the equally creative and destructive aspects.

After the primordial light was withdrawn there was created a 'membrane for the marrow,' a k'lifah husk or shell, and this k'lifah expanded and produced who was Lilith (Zohar 1:19b).

The shells of what becomes the hidden aspect of the Tree of Life, the Tree of Death, or Qlippoth hide the true nature of mankind. It is our attachment to the Earth and its more primal physical needs that we are expected to break through to find his inner divinity or spark of 'God'. So to be whole and balanced and truly divine one has

to 'ditch the shell'. Or at least that is how it could be perceived. Yet most on this Left Hand Path today would say not. To many it is a greater need to balance both the creative and destructive forces to blend the energies and to accept that both are necessary and have equal importance or else they wouldn't exist in the first place. But it is still not quite as existential or simple as this either.

Occultists such as Aleister Crowley and later on Israel Regardie saw the Qlippoth as not only representing the equally opposing side of the light side of the Tree of Life but also as both hurdles to overcome in order to reach deeper sources of divine knowledge and awareness and beings that represented the necessity for opposing forces in nature and 'God'. Each of the ten major influences or demons/angels on the Tree of Death relating to concurrent forces of 'Good' on the Tree of Life or Kabbalah. Here they are as placed from crown to root or earth.

KETHER / THAMIEL
EQUAL TO THE DUALITY IN GOD

Thamiel represents duality whereas the opposing perfect God head force of Kether represents unity. Thamiel is many not one as in Thamiel are forces/demons/angels who are also known as 'broken' or as Cathariel 'the fearful light of God'. In some respects Thamiel are seen as the pollution of God that sought to become more powerful and then fell from grace. Satan and Moloch reside here as adversaries of Kether, the unity and perfection of God. In some respects one can view this as a broken hologram still retaining the original form yet fragmented.

CHOKMAH / GHOGIEL

Where Chokmah is the masculine force of perception defined as motion so Ghogiel represents the antagonism to the well of creative

potential and eternal motion in Chokmah. Also known as 'The Hindering Ones'. Ghogiel wishes to block motion and kill the first seed of creation before it has a chance to germinate.

Fallen Angel Beelzebub / Beliel is also attributed here and often known as Lord of the Flies or those who feast on decay and death.

BINAH / SATORIEL

Binah is known as the intelligent feminine aspect of Kether, 'the mother' she gives shape and balances out the masculine force of Chokmah. Binah is also called 'the mother' and within her all formative forces rest which help shaping and balancing the creative potential of Chokmah.

Her opposing force, *Satoriel*, is the death of creative efforts to leave no-thing or nothing but lifeless form. Satoriel are the ones who conceal the true life essence of God. Sometimes these are also called '*The Hairy Ones*' the primitive forces lacking true souls and another link to Lilith's forces.

DAATH / BELIAL

Daath is often seen as the wisdom or knowledge gained by application of unified balanced forces working in harmony. Daath is a gateway and central pivoting point for the union of intelligent forces to make manifest creation. It can also be an egress and ingress route to both the light and dark side of the Tree. If Chokmah is father and Binah mother then Daath is son. Knowledge minus any desire for greed or power over others is required to pass through Daath. Selflessness.

Belial is the Qlippoth of Daath. This Force / Fallen angel can render knowledge useless and are sometimes known as '*The Worthless Ones*' so in travelling through this husk one must be aware of false information and be intelligent enough to spot it. One

must also not waste knowledge or its moment will pass rendering it of no value.

CHESED / GHA AGSHEBLAH

Chesed becomes the 'extension of divine will' it is the fourth Seripha and third triad on the Kabbalah. Otherwise known as 'mildness'. Here the results of the union of Chokmah and Binah are reflected in pure spirit. Where Daath is a 'son' or result of a union of forces and a resulting gateway so Chesed is the reflection of the previous forces at work. Her divine will is concentrated.

Gha agsheblah is the Qlippoth that seeks to thin and spread divine will so as to weaken it. Where the mildness of Chesed is loving and genuine so this Qliphoth represents weak love that will eventually fizzle out of its own accord through suffocation. Gha agsheblah are also known as '*The Smiting Ones*'.

GEBURAH / GOLOHAB

Geburah is seen as severity and is the fifth Sephira and the reflection of Binah in the Second Triad. Here the forces develop the forms that create justice in the world. The concentrated 'divine will' balances out the mildness of Chesed with the potential other extreme.

Golohab is the merciless reflection of Geburah it is the ultimate judge and able if necessary to destroy the creative life if needs be to restore balance. Golohab are known as '*The Flaming Ones*' purging and cleansing as required.

TIPHARETH / TAGIMRON

Tiphareth represents beauty and is the sixth Sephira and reflection of Kether in the Second Triad. This beauty is inner spiritual love and is akin to the heart in our body. It is the morality

and balance that creates harmony between Chesed and Gedburah.

Tagimron seeks to hide this beauty and to confuse the heart from finding its balance and harmony within pure spiritual gnosis. By creating states of confusion over love and the inner heart Tagimron will seek to conceal the truth by denying access to ones intuation by inferring doubt. Tagimron are known as '*The Confusers*'.

NETZACH / GHARAB

Netzach is the seventh Sephira and the first of the Third Triad. Here it is the second reflection of Chokmah and first reflection of Chesed representing the victory over opposing forces in nature. The birth of creation is unified here and expressed in its harmonious form.

Gharab is this stage minus the wisdom of Chokmah and mildness of Chesed. Therefore it is capable of destroying as easily as it creates without care or reason. Gharab are known as '*The Corrosive Ones*'.

HOD / SAMAEL

Hod is the eighth Sephira and the first reflection of Geburah meaning 'radiance'. It is the second reflection of Binah. Hod represents the concept of altered amounts or fluctuating concepts that multiply in our minds. Geburah concealed this as Binah founded it. The radiance of the light allows for states to alter and appear different.

Samael is the use of brilliance to blind us. Samaels force creates illusions. Here we can fool ourselves as well as others. Delusion and deceit lay here. This allows for negativity in our thoughts. Samael is known here as '*The Deceitful Ones*'.

YESOD / GAMALIEL

Yesod is the ninth Sephira and the last of the third Triad; it is

also the first reflection of Tiphareth and the second reflection of Kether. Here the positive physical manifestations required to create life are found. Here we find the sexual organs in the root of our life force. Here there is the potential to both attract or reject. Here natural balance and harmony is expressed in a healthy satisfying sex life that creates new life.

Gamaliel is unsatisfied sexual energy. Insatiable but barren unable to create from the energy. Lacking the inner spiritual beauty of Tipareth the energy and forces created will only end in destruction and exhaustion and ugliness in an inner context. Gamaliel is often known as '*The Obscene Ones*'.

MALKUTH / LILITH

Malkuth is the tenth Sephira and below the rest of the tree as a point. It represents the combined forces of all that is above. This feminine force is as an ultimate expression of all the energies needed to continuously exist in the 'kingdom' of Earth. Here all creative and destructive forces reach one position, or divine point , as above and so below.

Lilith is the culmination of all the preceding demonic forces above her. She is many in one. Sometimes also known as Namaah. She is '*Queen of the Night*' and is the 'disgracing spirit of nature', she seeks to destroy and break down forces rather than to create. But she is equally necessary and gives balance to the creative forces that all have to die at some point to allow new life. She is the pivotal shell surrounding the point of the God head or divine source.

And so here we return to Lilith and her parts to play in all our lives. I am not a trained Kabbalist or Qabalist, but new to this branch of mysticism. Having said this one can see how Lilith has evolved from the earlier demons and deities mentioned in Chapter

One to become the force the Hebrew people see as intrinsically evil and destructive.

Actually working spiritually with one or the other, and in some cases both, is something that requires dedication, devotion and trained mentoring. So whether your purpose is to develop and acquire greater knowledge and understanding of these mysteries or for some other reason such study requires a degree of self-mastery and it is not advisable to undertake it purely after reading a couple of books on the subjects. There is often a constant act of inner and outer reflection. And as each person is unique and will have their own individual personality so each person will take from these meditations and rites that which is pertinent to them. By seeing oneself in these mysteries it then becomes easier to decide which aspects are beneficial and which not. In some respects this is part of spiritual growth. In simplistic essence becoming more aware of self and our deepest motives and agendas one can then choose to either accept each one or move beyond it. The peeling back of the shells to reveal the underlying personality is not always a road that many people can travel with comfort and ease.

But it isn't meant to be easy. It is a true revealing and greater understanding of the commonness of human nature and how it is reflected in you. To drop or ditch the shell can also mean having to surrender ones ego self to gain access to deeper knowledge within. It also means coming to terms with your own destructive side. Once you are transparent to yourself then the divine core should be reached and from then on true enlightenment can occur as new growth minus ego attachments, in theory! Some see this as manifestations of ones 'higher self' but I prefer inner and outer self.

The need to explain the forces of evil and death evident in life came to a head in Jewish mysticism in 1492 with the expulsion of Jews from Spain. Later between 1534 and 1572 a man named Isaac Luria from Safed in Palestine sought to comprehend Gods ability

to cause such suffering to his so called 'chosen people'. One day the prophet Elijah appeared to him and said, "*I have been sent to you by the Almighty to bring you tidings that your holy wife shall conceive and bear a child, and that you must call him Yitzchak. He shall begin to deliver Israel from the Klipot / Qlippoth* (husks, forces of evil). *Through him, numerous souls will receive their tikkun* (free will and redemption). *He is also destined to reveal many hidden mysteries in the Torah and to expound on the Zohar.*"

Thus begun the revealing of the Qlippoth and development of Lurianic Kabbalah.

The Zohar also states that there is a *quaternion* marriage. The first pair are 'God' and his Shekinah. In Hebrew this word means 'dwelling place' which is often cited as meaning that 'God' could not exist without this female half of himself, hinting that 'God' or Yahweh/Jehovah was androgynous. It is also often thought that the last Hebrew Goddess accepted in the Temple, The Sea Goddess Asherah, was the consort. They were seen as ruling the celestial heavens above and Samael and Lilith had been cast down below to rule the Earth. It is also written that during the destruction of the Temple of Jerusalem that housed the Ark of the Covenant by the Babylonians, the House of the Shekinah caused Lilith to descend, and her handmaiden ascended becoming God's consort, thus showing her importance.

Although not proven or found in any Hebrew sources there are some that think the possible etymology of Shekinah evolved from Shakti a word for the divine feminine in Hinduism. Shakti is found as Lord Shiva's consort. The Hindus believing that this Shakti was the necessary home of the soul in God and or humankind. That there are parallels is obvious.

In the Zohar it is said that 'God' created two main luminaries, those of celestial light and those of fire. To put it as simply as possible 'God' is the masculine principle or Sun and the divine

feminine is the Moon. One rules the day and the other the night. Yet it is also said one was torn from the other and it is the constant lament of the Moon as it waxes and wanes that it cannot be truly as one with the Sun again. This places the female, in this case Lilith, as the one with most influence at night, hence pretty much anything of incidence that occurs during this time is apportioned to her energies, e.g. wet dreams, sudden infant cot death etc. It also explains the separating of the male and female energies. The founders of modern Wicca drew much from these ancient texts and used the underlying principle of balance between sexes to establish their premise that balance is always reflected in nature and therefore of supreme magical importance. And so Lilith and Samael are perceived as 'evil forces' on Earth in the minds of believers of the Zohar and are frequently the beings thought responsible for teaching humankind Witchcraft along with their son Cain. This is also integrated into many modern traditional paths. And although modern Wiccans venerate a Horned God and Moon or Earth Goddess often drawing from many polytheistic sources, the birthplace of the concept was essentially a Middle Eastern import and not necessarily much to do with any previous Paganisms found in Northern and Western Europe prior to its arrival.

So it is mostly to the Hermetic Qabalah that we must turn to truly discover the Lilith of Medieval times onwards. Here, along with others, we find both Lilith and Samael. Samael is seen as the Left Hand of God or the desolate aspect of divinity. And Lilith the elder is seen as Gamaliel who is deemed polluted of God and connected with the night time. She is the Queen of Demons and the demonic here is seen as evil or destructive rather than creatively inspiring although the real flip side is that these destructive and vile forces often spawn daimons that are new energy able to create and become whole and complete in the physical plane within Malkuth, the Kingdom of Earth. Hermetic teachings owe their wisdom to

Hermes Trismegistus who wrote his Hermetica which considers and employs the belief that there is one underlying divine being or God from which all others were born. This came at a time of polytheistic paganism and was perhaps an attempt to mix the concept of multiple lesser deities existing under the greater banner of a much larger whole or umbrella God. It isn't quite the same as monotheism but does manage to explain how the two can marry in the philosophical minds of ancient Greece and Egypt. Thoth and Hermes being seen as the same by many and the inspiration for Hermetic teachings and practitioners of the path usually advocate the use of astrology, magic, alchemy and the conjuring of spirits among other esoteric practices.

THE BLACK MADONNA

Some see this iconic image as representing Lilith. There are about 500 images discovered to date in the world most of whom can be found all over Europe, but more in France than anywhere else. In France there are 180 no less. Of her very little is known. Some see her as the figure head of a Magdalen cult that is often claimed to be a form of Gnostic Christianity whose mysteries travelled West with people such as The Knights Templer. This possible counter balancing side of the Virgin Mary seems to have sneaked in under the radar and is accepted as an alternative depiction of the traditional mother and child. You could be tempted to see it as, 'where there is one there has to be the other'. One pure, untainted and innocent the other a temptress whose deliberate actions stir the souls of men to constantly feel torn between what society expects of them and that which they feel more drawn to. Some have seen this as merely a desire by medieval iconographers to present a balanced view of the local population allowing for differing skin tones etc. and, therefore, still represents the Virgin Mary and the

Black Madonna by Gillian Macdonald

Christ child. And to be honest this does make the most sense. So the colour of the skin is not to be confused with a destructive 'dark' side more a hidden occult one. Considering most of the world does indeed have none white skin and if the Virgin Mary existed she would have been a Jewish Middle Eastern woman with off white colouring presenting her as a Black Mary is more accurate. Whilst others have interpreted them differently. Interestingly where they occur miracles are often attributed. Proponents of the belief that Mary Magdalene was indeed the wife of Christ frequently make a connection between the Black Madonna or Maria as the magical priestess and liken the imagery as Mary and the 'other child' or a literal offspring of Christ. This has become popular in modern fiction but lacks any definitive proof.

Churches dedicated to the Black Virgin are linked in with the princes of the Visigoths and anywhere having links with older pagan Goddesses who worked magic, such as the Goddess Freyja, and weaved. Symbols such as distaffs, crosses and the element of water are often found to coincide with these stories. Lilith is often depicted with the feet of birds, this alone links her with the air, flight and puts her forward as a contender for one of the inspirations of this cult. Another reason that Lilith could well have gained popularity and almost be seen as acceptable in the early medieval Church is due to her elevation as the consort of Yahweh, a title given to her by Cabbalists as they sought to reconcile the loss of Asherah and swapped the consort of Samael/Satan with that of God. To a non Cabbalist it can only be seen as a need for balance, the yin and the yang perhaps? Painting her as black skinned gave her a possible link with Sheba, to me these are all interrelated archetypes. Magical, mystical Maria's, they are The High Priestess of the Tarot and the Virgin Mary, the Empress.

Another story associated with Lilith that ties in with places in France where Black Madonnas turn up is that of Salome and her

mother Herodias. After they orchestrated the beheading of John the Baptist they were exiled to Spain, Salome drowned in a river but her mother and Herod the Tetrarch survived. It is written that from this a witch coven accused of child sacrifice sprung up and was established in the name of Diana Noctiluca, 'Queen of the Nighthags'. Strangely these children were killed in fields of flax only to be consumed and regurgitated before seemingly re-appearing in their cradles. Myths and folklores concerning deaths of infants have Lilith signatures. There are many Lilith stories in the Pyrennes where Herodias settled and these images of Black Madonnas also occur. But it is to saving, or resurrecting, the lives of children that the Black Madonnas became famed for. So here we could view it that the arrival of the Black Virgin was to give re-birth and new life where Lilith had chosen to inspire to destroy it.

Many ancient Pagan Goddesses have Lilith links and associations and could be seen as Black Virgins. If we begin with Ancient Egypt there are a few contenders who share similarities, Neith for example has been proposed as having Lilith qualities. She is the oldest of Goddesses and an inscription on her temple says, "*I am all that has been, that is, and that will be. No mortal has yet been able to lift the veil which covers me*". Sometimes called 'The Libyan' she is linked in with another name used by Lilith, Lamia and presides over the west the place of the dead. This eternally mysterious deity is self creating and self sustaining, much like Lilith. And as Nut she is queen of the night sky. But there are also those who would say that Sekhmet has Lilith qualities, she who destroys, and allows for decay to take place. Night time seasonal and ceremonial lantern processions where the Virgin is held aloft are traditional in many places to this day. One such is held in May and called 'the Gitan Pilgramage'. It takes place in Les Saintes-Maries-de-la-Mer and heralds back to St Marie-Salome's arrival from Palestine. This essentially Catalan and French speaking Gypsy tradition honours 'Black Sara' aka Black Madonna

as the patron saint of the gypsy community. Her statuette is held up accompanied by horsemen and dancing girls. Once the procession is over they are known for their rather heavy duty partying. And as with the English tradition of electing a May Queen the gypsies also have a living representative of Black Sara as their Queen for the Night. The following day they repeat the experience with both Sara's. It is a massive carnival drawing upon gypsies from many parts of Europe.

The Black Madonna is also associated with healing waters and sacred wells. In Greece those who practised the Eleusian Mysteries would hold night time torch lit vigils searching for Persephone as part of their tradition, this has also been associated with Black Virgins. And pagan Celts who worshipped Danu would make night time offerings in the river Danube.

For example, Goddesses such as the Egyptian's Neith and Sekhmet are also healers, they can give and take life. Lilith isn't usually accredited with healing powers and no houses of medicine have been run in her honour but she does have the original deity position and the destructive nocturnal one. Where Churches dedicated to the Black Madonna occur so do mystery schools of gnostic wisdom.

Dark skinned Goddesses would have been introduced into pre-Christian pagan Europe from the Middle East via Phoenician traders and one major contender for the title would have been Auset or as commonly known today, Isis. This Goddess is frequently depicted as sitting holding the infant Horus/Heru to her breast and is often carved from black stone. Back in 550CE in Soissons north of Paris there was a temple to Isis and it seems she was a accepted by local Celtic tribes. The Egyptian mythologies would have found their way to the Hebrew peoples and thence onto modern Christianity, indeed there are many who claim the one borrowed from the other. Classical Greece and Rome all had Goddesses that one could label

both creative and destructive or 'dark' whether in literal terms as in skin tone or their attributes and mythos. As did the Celts.

There are also those who would argue that a black or darker skinned Mary and Christ child is more authentic and that the subsequent white skinned versions were adopted as a way of making them more appealing to Western Europeans. And it would make sense. The tradition of hiding images of Goddesses in caves or underground chambers was a way of retaining a connection to older deities. The effects of Christianity sweeping across Europe and becoming the dominant religion was a stop start affair. Hanging onto the last vestige of Goddess worship through Black Madonnas is akin to Asherah being the last of the Hebrew Goddesses tolerated in the temple at Jerusalem. The demonising of Goddess worship and destruction of many Black Maddonnas allowed for the negative projection of 'evil' Lilith onto the image.

But it isn't, simply black or white, good or bad, the cult of the Black Madonna is more complex and indeed entire books on this subject have been written. To me she is a mixture of older dark skinned, often nocturnal, pagan goddesses and the Virgin and Child of Christianity. She is however predominantly a Catholic phenomena. One Church well known in France that has achieved much notoriety over its Black Madonna is Chartres Cathedral near to Paris. According to Julius Caesar this was built on a previous site used by Druids as a major meeting place and thought to also be a Neolithic burial mound.

Prior to the renaissance, or re-birth of interest in all things of classical and pagan antiquity in Europe, the earlier Medieval centuries had their Neo-platonic and Hermetic philosophies complimenting and challenging the religion of the day. But the Occultists of the renaissance took risks, they were often accused of Witchcraft and indeed some were hung for their practises. With their new books and secret writings came Lilith. As teachings such

as the Kabbalah became more readily available to those who could read and afford books so astrologers, philosophers, mathematicians and other such scientists of the time began to study occult magical ceremonial magic and created the foundations for what would much later become Western Mystery Schools.

RENAISSANCE LILITH

The concept of a succubus was written about in the 'Witches Hammer' or 'Malleus Maleficarum' in 1486 by Heinrich Kramer. And King James 1st the one responsible for ordering the translation of the Greek Old and New Testaments into English wrote his own book, 'Daemonologie' his view of succubus activity being down to a devil/demon stealing sperm from dead men and delivering it to women. The other view is that a dead man is risen and possessed and impregnates a woman. He also asserts that both succubus and incubus are both the same demons just able to switch sex. But he did agree that many cases were simply down to wet dreams.

One name that is synonymous with black magic and the summoning of demons is Cornelius Agrippa von Netesheim. Born in 1486 he was taught astrology by his father and believed that mastery over demons was essential for the advancement of the soul in order to become closer to God. The theory being that humankind must work with all the 'spheres' good and evil before they can achieve any state of near perfection. This desire to explain our place in the cosmos was at the root of much ancient classical gnostic training. He said, "*The magician gains power over the angels and ministering forces, and can manipulate them to produce worldly events. The higher the magician rises through the spheres and the divine world, the more powerful the angels which can thus be manipulated. The radical promise of ceremonial magic is fulfilled; demonic magic takes the soul to God*".

Queen Elizabeth I (artist unknown)

This sort of statement would still be considered controversial today among many who view any contact with demons as a negative or evil thing. So one can only imagine the risks people like him took in exploring such concepts back then.

Here in England during the reformation of the church brought about by Henry VIII great uncertainty befell the spiritual soul of the land. People loyal to the old church resisted the new Protestant replacement and all that it entailed. To some it was the negation of the Holy Mother. To others it represented a new door of opportunity temporarily opening as it seemed the tide of occult information, study and practise among Royalty, the rich and well educated was not to be abated just yet. To ordinary country folk it meant a turning back to folklore and sympathetic magical practises, including the hiring of Witches and cunning men. Putting their faith in previously tried and trusted forms of spiritual practise was a natural reaction to the breakdown of the Church of Rome's hold over the souls of England. The fear of the unbridled lustful demonic feminine pervaded however. And by the time of Elizabeth 1st's reign in England a new name arrived, that of John Dee and his friend Dr Edward Kelly.

Elizabeth herself was often called The Witch Queen of England. Born of Anne Boylen, a woman accused of coercing the King away from Anne's sister Mary who had an illegitimate child with Henry, her own desire to remain single and not marry was at odds with the times. Her constant battles to hold onto power and protect her country was her life's mission. She also consulted the mathematician and astrologer John Dee and employed him as court astrologer. He studied the Hermetic teachings and put many of them into practise in various countries in Europe including England. Born a Catholic he went onto study at St. Johns College Cambridge, an overtly Protestant College, and became a well renowned mathematician, astronomer, navigator, and for his time a cutting edge scientist as

well as a Catholic priest by the age of 26yrs. But it was his interest in the Western Mystery Traditions, particularly of classical Greece, Rome and Egypt that led him to become an adept magician and court astrologer to Queen Elizabeth 1st. Elizabeth was a highly intelligent well educated lady. She spoke several languages including Latin, was an accomplished musician, and avid reader among many other things besides. But it was her superstitious nature and interest in science and the occult that led her to John Dee. He taught her younger brother Edward for some time so would have been known to her. She placed much trust in him and his ability to foretell auspicious dates for occasions. Indeed, even the planned day for her coronation was decided by his augury.

During Elizabeth's reign Dee's influence seems evident in many places. Prior to the Witchcraft Act of 1583 anyone could be accused of witchcraft and various barbaric means were employed to discover the alleged truth. Ducking stools were commonly used and people tied to them and plunged under water in village ponds and lakes or rivers to determine their guilt. Should they survive they were guilty but if they drowned they were innocent. It was a veritable no win situation for those ducked. Torture was often used to extract confessions and unsurprisingly successful. No courts or judges were required nor was evidence. The Church saw to all aspects of charges of Witchcraft. Once the act became law it changed things considerably.

Now evidence was needed as were a court and a jury. People finally had a modicum of justice. Although the maximum sentence for anyone proven to have used witchcraft to kill was death by hanging it was rarely taken this far. And far lesser punishments were dealt out to any found guilty of lesser charges of witchcraft. During Elizabeth's reign no one was persecuted or tortured by the Church for witchcraft, the ultimate irony being that her act actually protected many from false accusations and it also saved many

innocent lives. She very cleverly managed to protect her own occult interests from Church accusations. But it didn't go down well with Pope Pius V who excommunicated her in 1570. Plots from Catholic sources to kill the heretic Witch Queen were to follow.

And just like Lilith, Elizabeth stuck to her chosen course in splendid spiritual isolation. Some surmise that coupled with John Dee and his deep esoteric knowledge Elizabeth was able to discover through magical means any threats poised against her backing up any of her own intelligence forces at the time. It has been suggested by some that scrying and necromancy were used by Dee in aid of Elizabeth but this is heresy and conjecture and cannot be proved. But she did visit his house in Mortlake in 1575 to see the astrologers 'magic glass'. We know this from Dees own diaries but he doesn't specify if it was a scrying glass or early form of telescope, either was possible. And earlier in 1572 a new star was observed that Elizabeth asked Thomas Allen and John Dee to verify and identify. This massive supernova in Cassiopia helped improve the science of astronomy considerably.

Elizabeth certainly had a cavalier attitude towards her own safety almost as if she knew she was covered. It is commonly believed that John Dee worked magic on numerous occasions to protect his Queen and patron.

Dee was well known for his interest in esoteric, Kabbalistic and occult knowledge. He was the one responsible for the birth of the Enochian Magical Tradition. But he wasn't very successful in his attempts to scry and so often employed the services of others. The name most people associate with John Dee is Edward Kelley. Kelley was a colourful personality of dubious character, indeed he had been found guilty of criminal acts prior to meeting Dee. Through Kelley Dee was able to connect with a spirit named Madimi. This child like cheeky and mischievous spirit often gave information and advice specifically for Elizabeth. To me this is a possible sign of Naamah

or Lilith the younger becoming involved without them really being aware of it at the time. But her transformation from sweet young virgin to shameless hussy takes the men by surprise as she orders them to share wives among other things besides. Madimi seems to control the spirits they invoke and instructs them men to begin using sex magic to gain knowledge. This is pure Lilith through and through.

The Enochian language was also channelled during scrying sessions with him and Edward Kelly. Believed by them to be the literal language of 'God' and described by them as the Angelic Language of the heavens they formulated a complex magical tradition around it.

Turning to many inspirations and sources including the 14th or 15th century *Key of Solomon* with its Goetic knowledge they delved into places considered dangerous by most at their time. They utilised the Aethama or seven pointed star of Babalon used by modern day occultists which was then known as the Great Pentacle. The book is divided into two sections containing magical instructions and sigils associated with angelic realms. This mighty grimoire might not have come to light had it not been discovered by Babylonions excavating Solomons tomb. And knowing Lilith's mythology this seems very pertinent.

They were particularly fascinated by the mention of The Whore of Babylon in Revelations concerning the end of times in the New Testement. A communication concerning this from 1587 goes thus;

"I am the daughter of Fortitude, and ravished every hour from my youth. For behold I am Understanding and science dwelleth in me; and the heavens oppress me. They cover and desire me with infinite appetite; for none that are earthly have embraced me, for I am shadowed with the Circle of the Stars and covered with the morning clouds. My feet are swifter than the winds, and my hands are sweeter than the morning dew. My garments are from the beginning, and my dwelling place is in myself. The Lion knoweth not

where I walk, neither do the beast of the fields understand me. I am deflowered, yet a virgin; I sanctify and am not sanctified. Happy is he that embraceth me: for in the night season I am sweet, and in the day full of pleasure. My company is a harmony of many symbols and my lips sweeter than health itself. I am a harlot for such as ravish me, and a virgin with such as know me not. For lo, I am loved of many, and I am a lover to many; and as many as come unto me as they should do, have entertainment. Purge your streets, O ye sons of men, and wash your houses clean; make yourselves holy, and put on righteousness. Cast out your old strumpets, and burn their clothes; abstain from the company of other women that are defiled, that are sluttish, and not so handsome and beautiful as I, and then will I come and dwell amongst you: and behold, I will bring forth children unto you, and they shall be the Sons of Comfort. I will open my garments, and stand naked before you, that your love may be more enflamed toward me."

This powerful visceral description of a creatrix Goddess certainly would have challenged the strong Christian control over England at the time.

Edward Kelly is reported to have invoked Lilith in 1592, the entity that came forth so terrified him that he never repeated the experience.

It seems that although both the world of science and the occult was a masculine only domain at this time in history, indeed it remained so for some time to come. It was ironically a female spirit who invoked the most fear in them. Women were seen as below men and only just above animals so having to serve both a Queen who would also be King and a girl child spirit who then became a harlot, must have been the ultimate "Ha! Had you!" to these men. Pure Lilith.

Earlier Bibles to the King James Version describe Lilith as Lamia but by the time she reaches the latter she has become the screech

owl. This is the only mention of her in this particular dubious translation from the Greek. And yet to many she did find her way to inclusion via Song of Songs. This alleged poem to the legendary Queen of Sheba is often thought to have been Lilith in disguise.

JACOBEAN WITCHHUNTERS

By the time of James 1st the reason women could not and were not tolerated as scientists or people capable of serious occult study was simple. Eve. All women were tarred with her brush. Eve was tempted by "The Devil/serpent" so women were weak and frail, not able to withstand demonic powers. Only men could be trusted to study such things and even then only within newly restricted parameters. To ensure his own views on Witchcraft were legally upheld he created the 1604 Act Against Conjuration and Witchcraft. Amazingly this more or less stayed in place until 1951 when it was replaced by the Fraudulent Mediums act. The vast majority of people accused and tried for Witchcraft were female. Those men wishing to invoke spirits could still do so as long as they stuck to "angels". This allowed for some play in proceedings and allowed for a certain level of activity to still be permitted, to some degree. It also allowed for Astrology but not combined with any form of spell craft. Only limited levels of divination were to be used.

His act stated a total ban resulting in the ultimate threat, the death sentence upon anyone who; "*Uses practises or exercises any invocation or conjuration of any evil and wicked spirit, or shall consult, covenant with, entertain, employ, feed, or reward any evil and wicked spirit to or for any intent or purpose.*"

England was now under a protestant King who having been inspired by a visit to Denmark and upon seeing how they were treating mostly women accused of witchcraft he took it upon himself to follow suit. Here we had a man who had become King who never

really seemed that comfortable with the opposite sex. His marriage hardly appeared very energetic. In fact he preferred the company of men. Not that this should in any way automatically lead to a lack of respect or fear of women. But it did. The scapegoating that followed was horrendous. Both genuine witches and those of less magical persuasions were tortured, sometimes by James himself, until they confessed their sins. His legacy continued and was exemplified during the English Civil War when characters such as Matthew Hopkins the Witchfinder General was employed ro seek out 'witches' and exact their confessions. This demonising of women, and searching in their most private of body parts, their genitals, for signs of the 'Devil's mark' became a sign that yet again women were under persecution. And it was a sexual issue. This attack on women was unfounded. The accusations were false and the inquisitions breaking out all over Europe in this era were horrific. The Church of Rome had upheld the sanctity of the Holy mother, of the married state and motherhood. This new regime was threatened by female power and knew how to quash it. Even seemingly respectable married women weren't free of prying eyes. Paranoia spread like wild fire and gave many a man fed up with his wife the chance to 'legally' off her with state approval. Got a woman locally owning property, sitting in the way of masculine power? Is her very existence blocking some plan to increase the wealth of her male peers? Then simply accuse her of Witchcraft and get rid of her.

Lilith and her promiscuous ways were under serious attack. Her children were hung for the most part and drowned, some even burned. The few genuine Witches who escaped would have had to maintained a level of nonreproachable respectability and pious religious observance and prayed nothing gave them away. Any regular magical practise put on hold or carried out only under the darkness of the dark moon with minimum of fuss. Spells chanted in silent whispers under their breathe and hoping above all else

that no one chose to point a finger their way or that, God forbid, they suddenly grow a new mole or wart, or worse have a house full of flies/imps. Cats were also persecuted. Often encased alive in chimney breasts of houses to ward off witches. Seen as Witches familiars they too were under attack. These were grim times.

The romantic renaissance of the Victorian era saw writers such as Johan Wolfgang von Goethe and his work, *Faust* in 1808 bringing Lilith to centre stage in our more modern psyches. As with the Zohar here she is Adams first wife and seen as a dangerous seductress. To quote from the book; "*Her beauty's one boast is her dangerous hair, When Lilith winds it tight around young men, She doesn't soon let go of them again.*"

The Art Nouveau and Arts and Crafts era was one born of romantic nostalgia and helped form the illusion of Avalon the misty Isle full of fae folk and Knights and damsels in distress but it also portrayed our erotic desires, especially the buried ones. And pale skinned long red haired maidens became the archetype for this Lilith. The temptress showing you her forbidden fruits, luring men with her mystery and her slightly wicked appearance makes her presence felt in the art of the time with people such as Dante Gabriel Rossetti the founder of the Pre-Raphaelite Brotherhood in 1848. He not only painted Lilith but his women folk were all red headed beauties with strong Lilith qualities. Dante Gabriel Rossetti originally painted Lilith. For some reason, in 1868, he changed the face from his original model to that of another of his favorite models. His main muse, Elizabeth Siddal was a pale skinned red head with long flowing locks and often modelled for other artists of the time. One of the most famous paintings of Lilith to which this poem is linked is of Elizabeth. Here he writes of her thus.

Of Adam's first wife, Lilith, it is told
(The witch he loved before the gift of Eve)

That, ere the snake's, her sweet tongue could deceive,
And her enchanted hair was the first gold.
And still she sits, young while the earth is old,
And, subtly of herself contemplative,
Draws men to watch the bright net she can weave,
Till heart and body and life are in its hold.

The rose and poppy are her flowers; for where
Is he not found, O Lilith, whom shed scent
And soft-shed kisses and soft sleep shall snare?
Lo! as that youth's eyes burned at thine, so went
Thy spell through him, and left his straight neck bent,
And round his heart one strangling golden hair.

Another famous poet, Robert Browning, wrote this poem on
her in 1883.

Adam, Lilith and Eve
One day, it thundered and lightened.
Two women, fairly frightened,
Sank to their knees, transformed, transfixed,
At the feet of the man who sat betwixt;
And "Mercy!" cried each--"if I tell the truth
Of a passage in my youth!"

Said This: "Do you mind the morning
I met your love with scorning?
As the worst of the venom left my lips,
I thought, 'If, despite this lie. he strips
The mask from my soul with a kiss--I crawl
His slave, – soul, body, and all!'"

~175~

Said That: "We stood to be married;
The priest, or some one, tarried;
'If Paradise-door prove locked?' smiled you.
I thought, as I nodded, smiling too,
'Did one, that's away, arrive--nor late
Nor soon should unlock Hell's gate!'"

It ceased to lighten and thunder.
Up started both in wonder,
Looked round and saw that the sky was clear,
Then laughed "Confess you believed us, Dear!"
"I saw through the joke!" the man replied
They re-seated themselves beside.

The contemporary spiritual currents of Lilith / Samael seem diverse and I don't feel it is right for any of us to lay claim to an ultimate path concerning them. As with most spiritual relationships with entities, deities, fae, ancestors, demons, angels etc. each is personal to the person involved. Traditions are tricky things to quantify. By definition the word implies longevity and a possible link to an older source. But all have to begin somewhere, and although there are those from ancient roots there are many more modern or contemporary cults and traditions that in future years will, no doubt, seem equally valid. There are tribal traditions, family ones, village or cultural ones and religious ones the list goes on.

Some are described as the LHP or Left Hand Paths of enlightenment and empowerment to reach a 'god like' divine state of being. One such example is Qabbalist especially those who incorporate the Qliphoth or hidden side of the Tree of Life. Indeed working with Lilith and Samael immediately places you in the darker realms of consciousness. Studying the Qabbalah or Kabbalah is often undertaken by mentorship and guidance of trained Western

Mystery School adepts. Such mentors are fairly rare. You may seek them or they might find you, either way the basic ground work leading to initiation and devotion has to be done.

Some are closed covens only open to initiates and magisters etc. within them. These contain souls with common purposes who aim to share spiritual experiences and learn and grow together through ritual work and other magical or sorcerous works. Lilith and Samael and their kin have quite a few existing today whose aim it seems is to devote time and effort into working with them.

And there are the solitary souls who have been touched by Lilith's flame and are on her path. These souls might well echo her own feelings of isolation and independence in their unique wholeness of being. In some respects this path is probably the hardest to navigate having no fellow sailors to aid the direction of the sails or tell when they a flapping and losing ground. The solitary path might well be a slower place of reflection of Lilith's mirror. But each to their own and it seems that if one is to work with others then they are sent your way and if alone one tends to always revert to this state of being alone even if brief interludes or encounters with other Lilith children are made.

There are also many on the Lilith current who find the energy an endless stream of inspiration for all manner of creative skills. Lilith is often found in the art and literary world, she also inspires dance and song. From Song of Songs and the Queen of Sheba to Dr. Who she is there.

LILITH AND THE MODERN WORLD OF BDSM

This world of sexual bondage and sadomasochism is often attributed to Lilith's influence and there are many that see her as the Queen of Dominatrix's. To me this would imply that there is a Lilith who always has to be in control sexually and maybe this stems

from the Ben Sirach version of the Garden of Eden? As was said in the first chapter, there are many Liliths. Here she would have to either be the Domina or the Submissive slave. And yet the role of the submissive does not seem to please any version of Lilith I have yet encountered. This does not rule out such a Lilith existing merely that she has not revealed herself to me. But another reason this world is equated with Lilith is due to Samael. There are many who see Samael as bound to the earth and in this I would heartily agree. But the image of Samael in black bindings with severed wings is also a common one 'seen' by many. This would indicate he is restricted from unleashing his full force upon us. And in essence this makes literal sense. As Angel of Death he could wipe out all life on Earth and many feel he would. It doesn't seem his desire or intent merely an incidental side effect of his energy manifesting on this plane. But by keeping him 'bound' Lilith can have access to him without him destroying her. This also resounds with the reference to Lilith not being able to have a 'normal' relationship. Hers is always a frustration, a partial involvement but never complete. But we know that in theory they have created children of their own, Cain being the first recorded example. And Azazel also, although some see him as Cain and some see him as Tubal-Cain. But that is a whole other book of it's own. So they are just as able to have offspring. As Angel of death he has to be able to allow new life or else there would be no purpose to him.

Going back to BDSM, this is more than games and 'play' though some enter into it this way. It is often deeply profound and intense. The level of trust required for it to work successfully as a way in which to unleash some of Lilith and Samaels energy cannot be understated. That they could and might possess during such activity is entirely possible should that participants be initiated or devoted to either spirit. And this can also involve past life connections so current devotions and initiations are not limited here. I speak from

experience and know how psychological this can become. It can also be extremely tantric in nature. As sessions can last a long time and orgasm is usually deferred or put off until last. A desire for such things is paramount or participants won't get much out of it. If this world and its mysteries arouse you then tread cautiously forward. But it is a game with rules for a reason. The emphasis is on consensual behaviour. Should either person wish to stop at any point it must be possible to do so. If any spiritual force is attracted to you during BDSM sessions then danger can potentially ensue. It is essential to either protect from such connections or if encouraged then have many ways of communicating during them.

Deep in this world people can experience many aspects of their sexual selves not easily opened by conventional sex. The desires to both dominate and control are in many respects superseded by the desire to give pleasure to the submissive. And some gain pleasure from both aspects of the dominant role. The desire to surrender and hand your body over as a play thing and source of arousal to the dominant is also superseded by the submissive gaining pleasure from the sense of over powering they are in receipt of. The sense of entering a world that up until relatively recently was taboo and secret and frowned upon by the mainstream has always been a tempting apple to bite into by those drawn to it. And again there is a similarity between pure and innocent submissive Eve allowing Samael and Lilith to have their wicked way with her.

Plus for many people pain is the key to arousal. Only once that level of endorphins is active can the person really become fully excited. The only problem here being that both Lilith and Samael are insatiable sexual forces and your own sex drive will be pushed to its limits by them. The need for you to gain control over this is as important here as it is with any form of potentially addictive activity. They will eagerly encourage addictions, of all sorts, particularly sexual ones.

To enter this world is to connect with part of their sexual mystery. It can be a far greater release of tensions and empowering raising self esteem and really work well especially if those trained in mystical arts bring magic into the session. But like most work with these forces it can also have the opposite effect. Should one partner only be doing it to please the other there is danger of lowering of esteem and potential depression etc. Unless it really does excite and arouse it is a world best left alone. It is perfectly possible to connect with Lilith and Samaels sexual energy through tantra, ecstatic union and lust without having to try BDSM.

Lilith is the raw primal creative and equally destructive nature of nature.

She is the Judaic evil, the Sumerian Priestess and the earliest prototype Goddess of Anatolia akin to Hekate.

She is the night time, the moon light, the menses, the perils of childbirth and the destroyer of infants.

Mother of Demons, Queen of the Night, Sister of Lucifer if Lucifer be Venus, and consort of Samael the Angel of Death and serpent of the Garden, the secret hidden or occult key of Solomon the Whore of Babylon, she is the feminine survivor of Asherah.

That the wild, free spirited independent woman will eventually rise from the ashes is every child of Lilith's hope.

Chapter 5

Working with Lilith

Lilith's universally agreed upon unpredictable nature leaves her free and yet restrains us from being able to set in stone just how anyone should go about working with her. Your experience will be yours, unique and personal to you. Having said this, and after sharing with others on her current, I have found some commonalities that seem to permeate her wake. I call it a wake as she can leave you either feeling as though you might capsize or at the other extreme awaken you to a sense of spiritual enlightenment.

Firstly Lilith will choose you. You may feel drawn to her but take note of what exactly drew you to her. This might well be your starting point or it might just be the aspect of Lilith that she wants to alert you to at this time. Chances are that she is calling you whilst giving you the illusion of thinking that it was in some way your own personal choice to be inspired by her. Only you can truly delve into this inner plane. Only complete honesty with yourself concerning you true nature, no matter how wonderfully revealing or horribly uncomfortable, will help you understand why. I am not about to suggest any reasons or explanations. You have to be prepared to be brutally open with yourself on a level that might, or might not, be uncommon to you. She will laugh at any denial and allow you to keep seeing that reflection until you acknowledge it. What you choose to do about it then, is up to you.

As a lady of liminal spaces she awaits us at liminal times. As we both drop off into sleep and just before we awaken, she is there. If in

a cave which is neither land nor sea, there she sits. If watching the sunset and night fall, then she descends. All halfway points in life are hers including the moment of birth and death.

Let us look at some of her qualities that have already been mentioned in this book from a personal spiritual growth perspective.

Starting with her oldest possible reference as Lili, Lilu or Lilitu, she is the Akkadian storm demon.

So we have an energy that has destructive potential. It can be frightening. It is of the air. But like it or not it is a force of nature. Storms come in varying types. Most of the storms this Lilith stirred up would have been sand storms. So she would cover everything in sand causing dramatic chaos in her wake. Opening up a portal as she does. She is first and last. Beginning and end.

And so we can expect our relationship with Lilitu to occasionally be like this. She will, when she feels fit to do so, stir up a sudden unexpected storm in our lives. She will bring temporary chaos. She will change the appearance of ordinary things. Our lives will be altered in some way by this aspect of her energy. Now many would argue that this is merely a spiritual response to our own deeper needs. And others might say that it refers to something she feels is required, either way it might feel like the Tower card in the Tarot. That which is not set in stone in your life is under threat. Any weaknesses are exposed. You are left feeling vulnerable. Look at what is left to work with in your life and stick to what feels safe and secure. Only rebuilding over again is the answer. Accept that it has happened, find reason if you can and move on. This Lilith is raw, transforming and fast, very fast. Those resistant to any type of change are likely to suffer the worst with this aspect of Lilith if she manifests her stormy energy in your life. Only by either accepting and surrendering to the change or actually embracing it can you hope to recover from it.

Next we will look at working with the Ardat-lili this Lilith is the

first recorded succubus. Here Lilith is working with both storm and sexual energy. Her prime goal here is to take the seed of men. In many cultures this seed is seen as the life giving force. By taking it she temporarily exhausts the man. This also provides this Lilith with the missing element she requires to create her demonic brood. So she sweeps in suddenly by night whilst the man sleeps, inspires him into having a sexual fantasy and then steals his seed at the moment of ejaculation. This Lilith gave people at the time an explanation for wet dreams. As mentioned earlier this can of course be explained away by sleep paralysis combined with imaginative fantasy. But if you have experienced it then it is terrifying. Having the feeling that a physical presence is in the bed with you when you know for sure that no one is there is scary. Especially if it is mixed in with being aroused. This would mess with most people's minds. But it is a part of Lilith to do this.

Looking deeper into it we see that she is provoking men and, if taking the role of succubus, then women also into revealing their sexual desires to her, and themselves. She brings this energy to the surface so no matter what they are she will inspire you to focus on them. She might encourage you to try and act them out. This might be a wonderfully enriching and enlightening experience or it could flip the opposite way and have a negative effect on you. It might also be seen as wrongful or illegal in your society, Lilith is unlikely to care about this. But she will be interested to see how much she can influence you and how strong your own self-preservation is. And it is entirely up to you to make any decisions based on your own morals and ethics about how far you would go to express your sexual self be prepared to live with the consequences. This is in part what she hopes for. She wishes to get people to move beyond being frightened. She aims to get you to fall in love and lust with her through these visits. Then she can activate her inner vampire and use you as a source of food. So great care is advised in how much

of this relationship you allow to occur. Gaining conscious control over it and only allowing it to happen on your terms is a way of either putting her off you or gaining her respect. If she really does love you and wish to feed from your energy then make sure to take some of hers in return. Once a two way reciprocal relationship develops, and they are very rare, then a greater price might have to be paid. For this Lilith is a jealous lover. She will not allow you to love a mere mortal as deeply as you love her. This Lilith will encourage promiscuity but only on a free spirited none attached way. Be warned.

Ardat-lili is a sign of the next step in her evolution. As we have already explored, according to the myths she has it in for pregnant women and young infants. As a spirit unable to be fully manifest and incarnate she is unable to bare children in our manner. The tendency here might be to see her as a jealous barren woman. But I think not. This Lilith is deliberately trying to reduce our numbers. She seems to loath babies and pregnant women. Yes, this is harsh and cruel. But again people needed ways of explaining and yet again apportioning blame for pregnancy related deaths and sudden infant ones including still births. All these unhappy events are blamed on beings such as Ardat-lili, Lamashtu and Lilith. But the reflection here could also be that there are powerful natural forces of destruction in nature that are there to help keep balance. She is justice, justice is the scales, and the scales don't always balance out the way we want. Because it is not always about what we want or what we see as just. Lilith sees the bigger picture. She sees us as a mere part of life on this planet. And as such why should we be treated any differently.

This Lilith challenges both men and women to come to terms with negative aspects of the dangers and responsibilities of creating life. She installs fear in us all with the dread that it might not turn out well. Most women have terrible dreams of losing babies when pregnant and after they are born. And this ancestral genetic

memory is both incredibly powerful and also very hard to move our modern mind beyond. Here in the developed world where access to medical intervention is possible high levels of infant and child mortality has been greatly lowered. In poorer countries this is not the case. And yet in spite of this imbalance our numbers are still increasing dramatically to unsustainable levels.. It is sad to me to think that our love for our offspring and our desires to protect them might eventually be our undoing. For as our population expands way beyond what the planet can sustain Lilith is watching and seeing the ultimate irony in our fear of her actions. For she knows that in many ways it might have been easier in the long run to blame her for the deaths even if there were way more of them again, than to sit back and struggle with a future where the only ones to blame for not being able to survive on this planet will be us.

In her next possible incarnation she is the Sumerian and Assyrian Goddess Ninlil, Lady of the Air, also known as Mulitu she has a consort Enlil. In this myth Lilith is a virgin raped whilst by the river Nippur after rebelling against her mother's wishes and swimming in it. The rapist Enlil is banished by the Goddess Ereshkigal in the underworld for his crimes. Here this possible Lilith is the defiled virgin. This is one who has either allowed herself to be in a dangerous position or thinks she is above being a target of it. Either way she is raped.

This Lilith doesn't seem to fear her rapist, she chases after him. This would imply that she was angry rather than frightened but her goal seems to be to pin him down to matrimony. It seems to pay off though as eventually after he has fooled her with several different disguises she becomes his wife. She gets her goal, such as it is.

But in other accounts the meeting is less violent and very much described as a sacred and possibly tantric experience. These extremes of sexual encounter are at odds with one another and yet this Lilith seems to be saying that all is a part of human nature

whether we like it or not. Societies laws change. Moral and ethical boundaries on sex and marriage vary from culture to culture and alter constantly throughout history. Many myths are written and in some cases re-written to accommodate this. In the second story she is also celebrated as the one who always achieves her desires but this time it is from making love, indicating that here the female orgasm is being highlighted as a good thing.

This Lilith is getting us to look at the extremes of our desires. She is asking us to explore how raw lust can arouse primal energy and that this can both be destructive and terrifying but in some is arousing. The line is a fine one however. She wants us to be honest about this. She certainly refuses Adams insistence at her taking the traditional missionary position in sex but this doesn't necessarily mean he was attempting to rape her. It seems that in ancient Mesopotamia rape was a punishable act and the myth serves to enforce this concept in the minds of any men who might consider such action. For if the high council of the Gods punished Enlil then surely they will also punish mortal rapists. But she also seems to be saying that a cunning rapist, like Enlil, will still be able to fool women. He will do it again as it is his nature to do so. In Ninlil's case by getting Enlil to truly fall in love with her she calmed his violent tendencies and gave him a safe outlet for his desires and in so doing he rewarded her with orgasms. And who is to deny that this occurs daily in humanity? We constantly hear of young girls and women being forced into marriages against their wills and being raped, this still occurs to this day.

Here she says men can be violent in their attraction for you. Sex and death are linked. The rise of testosterone is powerful sometimes, it can be damaging, lethal, dreadful but not always. This extreme of sexual behavior is deemed a negative illegal act in most cultures and most women would prefer to avoid it at all costs. Lilith however does not fear the rapist. She would turn on him, she would

drain him of his energy, she would search him out and fool him into thinking he has had his evil way. This is very much an aspect of Lilith. Lilith loves taboos. She is one.

The second story of Ninlil seems to be suggesting to men of that time that there is another way. You don't have to force yourself on women to get them. You can seduce them with flowers and poetry, you can lure them to beautiful places and make love to them and they in turn will reward you by showing their appreciation and give you their orgasm.

The poem relating to this story in chapter one is even more revealing of our sometimes hidden nature. A man will often pursue a virginal girl with lust in his loins. This is, in many, his nature. A virginal girl may or may not allow this man to catch up with her. She will often run from his advances. He might still choose to take her by force. She might find she is hurt and terrified of this or quite the reverse that she is aroused by him. Either way once his semen has entered her womb it is also registering on a spiritual level. His creative life force is inside her. It will go above to the heavens, and down to the netherworld. It will exist now on all planes. Once a woman falls for a man she will often pursue him. And Enlil is constantly meeting other girls and asking them not to give his whereabouts to the following Ninlil. Is he simply turned off by her now avid interest in him? Or is he wishing to avoid taking responsibility for his previous actions? It seems that this myth in both cases touches very briefly on the reactions to attractions in both sexes.

Even to this day Lilith is showing us that the complexities of our perspectives on rape are causing some painful deaths to occur. Thankfully most of our Western cultures see it as a serious crime and if proven carries a prison sentence for the perpetrator. But sadly in some cultures the woman is the one punished for being raped. It is as if she is blamed either for causing it in the first place

or allowing it to happen. The men who do the raping seem to be getting off scot free. In some respects things seem more unfair now than ever before. And a free spirited sexually promiscuous child of Lilith has no place in these cultures or is the one being blamed for causing the men to act in this way, even to this day! Lilith also seems to be drawing our attention through Ninlil and Enlil here in saying that we should be wary of our law makers and the punishment they deal out. And yet she also knows that women can scream rape but be lying about it and use this as a tool to punish a man for something else she feels hurt by. The complexities of this subject are many it seems.

So this aspect of Lilith urges us to delve into all our fantasies and desires and be honest with ourselves over them. Once we can accept our true sexual nature and be at peace with it then we can express it but always with the laws of our land kept strongly in mind and the ability to live with the consequences of our actions. Only when we repress or deny our true sexual nature are we risking damaging ourselves or others. And if our desires are illegal then we have to find a safe outlet for this energy.

Next to a very dark Lilith, Lamashtu. Here we meet the baby killing Lilith. This one will take the unborn and the recently born. In order to take the unborn it is believed that she touches the pregnant belly of the mother seven times to have her disastrous effect. But again this is never as black and white as painted. Most pregnant women are happy to be pregnant and hope for a healthy baby. But not all. Some regret being pregnant and secretly wish for Lamashtu to visit them. In our Western culture abortion up to a certain number of weeks is legal but not in all. Catholic women are not supposed to have them for example. Many pregnancies are a surprise and not planned and, getting back to Ninlils story, some are the product of rape. So Lilith is prepared to help us look at this more honestly. But again Lamashtu does not really care. She is not

judge or jury, she seems indiscriminate in her actions.

It is this demon Goddess's nature to do what she does. If she were a piece of software in a computer then this would merely be how she has been programmed. She knows no better. She is driven by her lust for the death of women and babies. It is as simple as that no matter how unpleasant and uncomfortable that might sound to us.

Here Lilith asks us to examine our own view on pregnancy and babies. Are we happy at the thought of becoming parents at some point? Have we ever harbored thoughts of wishing death on anyone who is pregnant or any unborn or young child? Most of us haven't but some have and do. Is there really a place for this Goddess in our psyches? Can we accept her horrible role as being part of what was, until we found ways of out maneuvering her, a natural state of being?

But Lamashtu is even worse by all accounts. She is also a blood sucking vampire who feasts on the flesh of humankind. So not only is she killing off women and children she is also capable of devouring men. The diversion from killing women and children to becoming a serial killer with cannibalistic blood lust to boot seems an elevated reaction to the fear this Goddess invokes. One can imagine how these stories spread and grew. Fear fuels fear.

Lamashtu urges us to look at how our fears grow and manifest when we don't have obvious answers or understand the reasons for things happening that upset and frighten us. If we wish harm to our own fetus or that of another women we need to look at why. It is not for us to judge ourselves but to try and comprehend where the underlying fear came from that provoked such a reaction. Only by addressing our deepest fears can we move beyond being part of a blame mentality. She also shows us how one fear can lead to another and how in being frightened of one terrible thing occurring we are in danger of actually making worse fears occur. She is a potent

warning against fear generally.

But Lilith is pressing home once more; ' ... *in a mortal sense I am barren, not like you, I am always to be slightly out of sync with humanity, my kin are my family. I have the ability to protect you against all odds and dangers, I can bring new life into your life, but I will also be there at the deaths, sexually I will attract many but can do little in a normal sense. I will tease and taunt and play mind games with you, this is a part of my nature.*' And yet in this poem it saddens her to be this way. She is at odds with her own nature. And it is a nature she knows she cannot change.

HEBREW LILITH

Many aspects of Lilith have evolved to create the Hebrew Lilith or Queen of the Night. This echoes the Burney Relief. Here she is also linked with owls. And being nocturnal hunters this is not surprising but they are a generally accepted spiritual sign of wisdom also.

Her greatest wisdom comes to us by night.

She is the Lilith of the Zohar, the temptress/harlot. Looking at both the times and places accredited with the creation of the Zohar provides interesting clues. In 200 BCE Israel and particularly Jerusalem had fallen under the rule of one of Alexander's previous generals who promoted and pushed for Hellenistic pagan worship to be observed. So if the prophet Elijah was inspiring the writing of the Midrash's at this time it might have been in reaction to this happening. Equally if it was purely created by Moses de Leon in Spain whilst Spain was Islamic then it might well have been in reaction to this. Neither religions were Jewish.

That it is brilliant in its conception is undeniable. To truly delve into the study and actually make it a life's work to comprehend the inner mysteries of the system is a daunting task. That it has divine inspiration is unquestionable. The Kabbalah describes

the separation of divinity from its creation, the universe/s, and reflects in our own inner separations. Our conscious mind is not in synchronicity with our subconscious, our nervous systems are two major types, sympathetic and parasympathetic. It works on the principle that 'God' cannot be contained in this physical vessel, or universe as we see it and know it. These were very clever ways of trying to understand and comprehend the mysteries of the spiritual and physical universe. The Good and Evil that the Tree of Knowledge imparted to us is the awareness of this separation. That once you bring conscience into consciousness you move from the instinctive and intuitive and bring cognitive forces into play. The creation or Big Bang is the explosion into squillions of fragments that occurred once 'God' or the brain, decided to create.

As Moses de Leon would have been well versed in the Torah and all Jewish scriptures he had inspiration from ancient times to draw on. So regardless of who or what inspired and for what purpose for this book it is only important to focus on why Lilith is suddenly so prominent and important.

Lilith is described in the Qliphoth as being the shell or husk that covers the brain. This is a very strange abstract concept. For we all have skulls covering our brains but if we put this in a spiritual context then it must relate to how she covers clear thinking. She creates the dream space. If this does indeed connect and is a medieval attempt to describe dreaming then it makes far more sense. She governs the subconscious and as most dreaming occurs at night and is linked in with darkness in our collective consciousness then this also applies to Lilith. Dreams are surreal they are a mixture of our conscious input with all kinds of other energetic influences. She is the night hag, the night mare, the nasty dream that suddenly frightens us. This is all a part of Lilith. The mix of energies earthly and spiritual is a key and accentuates the liminal half space they occupy. They can be on both planes simultaneously, they can be doors, catalysts,

and portals to either realm should they wish to be.

Many people view the divine as above, out of reach, the Kabbalah does this also and the crown is the God head. Lilith is placed at the root, here on this earthly plane. To bring Lilith's energy comfortably into the Kabbalah it is necessary for us to place her in the belief system of monotheism. Here there is an ultimate creator God. This God is all, is everything, Lilith is a part of this God. So to work with the Hebrew Lilith this has to be taken into account and if you are, like myself, a polytheist, it's a difficult one to work with.

But the world that this Hebrew Lilith evolved from was not monotheistic. It became that way. Her roots were in polytheistic pagan traditions. So what is this Hebrew Lilith going to teach you? Only you can know for sure. To travel the Qliphoth is one option. By studying this you could, in theory, walk the hidden to arrive into the light. The true light has little to do with the light that we get from the sun. This light is more the light of illumination. It is a light that reveals, to seek new light in the darkness of our own souls is to seek greater awareness and understanding and the real wisdom that come with it. So in effect it is inner light. Anyone who has crossed the abyss and seen the heavens as they really are will know that in many respects spiritual wisdom can throw acquired scientific knowledge out of the window.

Perhaps the best way to work with the Hebrew Lilith is to balance her out either with Samael or Lucifer. To choose Samael when wishing to bring sex magic into the equation and Lucifer when some higher illumination or wisdom is wished for. But don't underestimate the fiery power here. Ask for the energy to flow through you but not harm you.

The revolving of the flaming sword that guards the Tree of Life has her fleeing. She is not accepted in this garden. Only the Tree of death and Knowledge are accessible to her. Lilith is not permitted to visit the Tree of Life. The flaming sword turns and shows her that

only by accepting her own death can she gain access here. She is not yet ready for this. And so even though her consort is the angel of death, they can cast it upon us but not themselves. Death is with them but evades them. This dichotomy seems strange but in essence to me it points out the obvious, that death has to exist.

So facing your own mortality and becoming at peace with death and releasing the deep primal fear associated with it is also a massive part of working with Lilith and Samael.

CRONE LILITH

She wants us to look at our relationships with groups, tribes, clans, kin, peers etc. She is often drawn to those who are emotionally independent and solitary by nature. Her children are the rejected ones, the ones who either feel abandoned or those who choose to be alone. She understands the need to feel a part of a family but asks us to explore the possibility that potential families take many forms. She ends up having to create her own. She adopts various fallen angelic beings and creates new ones. She is a matriarch, a grandmother. A true child of Lilith will value her family but accept that her blood kin or biological birth family might not be the ones she ends up lavishing the most love, time and energy on. In this she wants us to be open to the prospect of doing the same. 'Family' (as in the one you are born into) are not always people you actually find you have much in common with. So keeping an open mind on this matter is very much a part of this message I feel.

It seems she could also be saying that no matter how you start out in life things change and adapt. Be prepared to be judged and rebuked, suffer, bare all this and eventually no matter what role you get you will be rewarded.

The Holy Spirit that is both the acceptable mother face of the divine feminine in Asherah is liminal neither here or there, not one

thing or another, but her energy can be used to both create and destroy once you see her hidden face, the crone Lilith.

The crone aspect of Lilith is often the most terrifying, she is icy cold, cutting and direct, she does not waste any time. She isn't one to be messed with. She is in some respects the bad tempered old lady at the end of the street, akin to maybe Baba Yaga. Her mysteries are complex and born of an eternity of wisdom and experience. She helps us face old age, to find comfort in losing ones youth and adapting to the changes in our physicality. She bares scars. And loves to tease the young men as the succubus rearing up on them as the night hag. As crone she wants us to drop preconceived ideas about how older women should conduct themselves. She wants her crones to relish in losing the monthly cycle and all it has entailed for a large part of their lives. She wants us to still embrace a sexuality regardless of how our outer appearance might be changing. She doesn't care for model grandmothers, she wants rebel grandmothers teaching their grandchildren to have adventures, think for themselves, work out their own morality. She rebels against the socially acceptable face of the older woman, she says "dress how you like", "speak your mind", "live life to the full". And most of all she wants us to know that as crones we can all, if we wish to, have the last laugh.

WORKING WITH CONTEMPORARY LILITH

I have not as yet met anyone who has been called by Lilith and has acknowledged it who is not already a witch or on some sort of pagan/occult path. But should this not be the case I hope to include here the very simple basics. Now, many might well say at this point that Lilith is hardly an introductory level being. But my view is that if it is Lilith who is knocking on your door then she is your first contact and as such it helps to know a little of her and how best to approach working with her. By working we mean to enter into a spiritual relationship, this will, like any relationship require

a two way communication. This might sound peculiar. And if you are unfamiliar with what it means to enter into bonds, pacts and relationships with spiritual beings then it is really important to grasp what this will mean to you. It means that you will eventually be able to invoke her deliberately and make pacts, acquire guidance and wisdom, gain protection, maybe get some results of magical endeavors among other things, and both your spirit and hers benefit from this. But it also means that she will get into your head, and influence your life as she sees fit, and often when you dig deeply enough you'll find things that subconsciously you desire or wish for.

This often tends to be the case with any deity, spirit, angel, demon etc. that you devote any long term time to. So if the thought of this puts you off then don't call on her. Spiritual callings are relationships are like any, they require that you give them regular time and energy. I know of some that call on specific deities on certain dates to honour particular festivals and seasons etc. but don't take it to the next level. Which to me is like attending the party of a friend of a friend and expecting some sort of amazing magic to occur, it might, but more often than not it won't. Lilith is intense, soul possessing, she is deep and rarely takes kindly to being ignored for too long. I have known her to both refuse to answer potential initiates and also kick those she does still need in her life for some reason well and truly up their posteriors if they fall foul of laziness or complacency. She is what I could describe as moderate to high maintenance. And although in this day and age it would be great to drop sexual differences and say that she is pretty much the same for both men and women, this doesn't seem to be the case.

Then there is the Right Hand Path versus Left Hand Path route with Lilith. The first being more one of inner wisdom, spiritual growth, and sacred sexual congress and the other leans more towards liberation, malefic practise and if sexual more lustful. To be honest Lilith herself doesn't recognise any path. This one always goes off the path. I tend to view her as more left than right but she

can, and often does ,inspire you to work both ways.

Now to condense basic magical instruction/training into a chapter at the end of a book is ludicrous, it can't really be done, I can really only hope to skim the surface and advise that serious apprentices seek more in depth guidance.

As a child of Lilith you are of witch blood, you can use, adapt, and create your own rituals, all paths and traditions might have something to offer you and Lilith is always there. So although there isn't really a 'right' or 'wrong' way of doing things it would help to establish your own personal boundaries with her. Lilith inspirations can be extreme. And occasionally, illegal. And unless you wish to be incarcerated for following through on one of her whims then make sure she is very aware of how far you are prepared to go. One way of getting around this and allowing some of the more risky suggestions or requests she plants to come to fruition is to express them creatively. Lilith loves to inspire in this way, from writing to art, dance, music etc. she is happy as long as there is an outlet.

And as most magical systems have commonalities it is often best to go and find them. See which elements are in most of the old tried and tested traditional magical methodologies. Most ritual constructs have an underlying infrastructure that can be adapted to suit Lilith.

I will say however, that if you are planning on utilising your magical skills purely for selfish gain you will almost definitely come a cropper. To use magic in this way does work but it lessens the connections you are going to get to those who are only out for what they can get from you. If you wish to spend all your magical life purely making pacts, giving offerings and receiving rewards be careful what you wish for.

BASICS

1 *Meditation/Visualisation* - Learning to calm and still the mind is essential for virtually any magical practitioner/witch. Once a certain level of self mastery over thoughts is acquired then it will make

any magical work more effective and your own connections easier to achieve. So learn at least one form of meditation and meditate regularly. Lilith loves mind games so it is absolutely essential not to miss this vital step towards working with her. Then you will be able to differentiate between right thinking and wrong/paranoid thinking.

A simple method is to choose a time when you won't be disturbed, wear comfortable clothing, avoid lying down you might risk falling asleep and find any position that is easy to maintain for at least 20-30 mins at a time. Light a candle and some incense if it helps. This goes for all forms of meditation. Now shut your eyes and focus on your solar plexus and your breathing, keep your mind focused on your breathing, if your mind wanders forgive it and return back on your breathing. Note any shift in the speed, depth and sound of your breath, also you might realise your nostrils alter in dominance when breathing. Once you are breathing in a relaxed regular manner focus the attention of your mind to your third eye. Imagine someone is pressing a coin around the size of a 2p piece there. Though this will become less required as you progress. Imagine inside your head at this point there is a light getting brighter and brighter, by doing this you are activating your pineal gland. Make a note what colour becomes a dominant one for this light. Next time you do it merely focus on seeing that light. This aids your psychic abilities. I am not going to waffle on about chakras, they are largely misunderstood by many in the Western world and seem to have been simplified down to a basic 7 that are easy for people to remember. As it is they are energy centres/nodes in our bodies and are many. They can also move about. It will help to learn to channel and draw upon various forms of energy in order to work more effectively with her.

Once you have been practicing this regularly for several weeks then try some simple visualisation exercises. I feel that it is important to be able to visualise when practicing any magical work. Connecting

with your own inner mind is imperative for generating a positive connection spiritually. Old school methods advocate creating inner 'temples', now here Lilith might differ. I've not found Lilith a great fan of 'temples' of any description. Caves, trees, desolate places yes but not Temples. So with Lilith in mind I sometimes use a cave. The cave is a place she is happy in. Learning to visualise a cave you can meet her in will always be useful. Again, if the mind wanders just bring it back to your chosen point of focus.

The next level of meditative exercise is to use it in order to raise magical energy. This is essential. Do your basic relaxation technique, visualise your cave and now imagine roots growing down out of your feet into the ground, see these roots going deep into the underworld. Down to the place of the dead, Lilith's consort is death, working with Lilith will be practising a form of necromancy or nigromancy at times so being able to draw energy from willing ancestral spirits is always an honourable and useful spiritual thing to do. But for now we are simply drawing energy from the place of the dead rather than any specific spirits. Pull this life giving energy up, see it as black energy rising up your legs filling your body with warmth. Don't be put off from this, the dead decaying warm soil is what gives birth to new life, there is nothing to fear from this. And now focus on your sexual organs and tail bone let the energy pool here start to see it turning red extending outwards into your aura/ energy field. But try raising the red up through entire body from root to crown this will help activate your inner witch fire. If the seed is there lying dormant it will respond to this and begin to cultivate or grow each time you meditate on it. Once the fire reaches your third eye focus it as a candle or flame, here it will help open your ability to 'see' on inner planes. Stay within the cave whilst doing this and you will be safe from any spiritual entity drawn to your new flame. With more of a Right Hand Path it is fairly normal practise to draw white or celestial energy down and then either circle both

streams around your body or twine them in a similar pattern as a caduceus. But raising Lilith energy is simply that, raising. It comes from below. Once invoked it can be anywhere and all around you.

If you wish to bring Lucifer's energy into the meditation then by all means focus on white light and create a circle of energy below, above and all around you.

For the purposes of working with Lilith, and to some extent becoming a more adept practitioner of the mystic arts, it helps to master the ability to switch in and out of differing states of consciousness. Only through daily meditations and visualisation exercises can you cross the divide and be able to direct your mind to where you wish to be. A heightened state of intuition and psychic sense should naturally increase the more you do this. There are several forms of meditation and if you try some you are bound to find one that works well for you. To work effectively you need to reach a point where you can drift in and out of trance states with ease. This allows you contact to inner planes and a space known often as the void or abyss from which all planes can be accessed. If you are of Witchblood then it should come relatively easily for you unless you are blocked in any way. Certain traumas, especially childhood ones, can do this and some medications will also. But as an exercise try this. Imagine you are back sat at school, you've switched off, the lesson is boring, you began by thinking of something else prominent in your conscious mind and found yourself drifting, soon you are deep in your subconscious visualising and letting your imagination take you on a journey, you are day dreaming. This is the precursor to trance. As you do this go in your mind to a place of wildness, a forest, moor, heath land or the like. See a mist all around your ankles slowly rising, feel the air grow colder, wish to be lost in this place and drift further into a semi-sleep. If successful this simple exercise should take you into a light trance state. Here it is easy for Lilith to make contact with you. It is also a generally

useful skill to master as most spirits including those of the dead can connect with us at this level. For deeper trance then repetitive chanting, humming, rocking can lead you there as can ecstatic dance as do some hallucinogenic recreational drugs of course. Though that is potentially a dangerous road to take as parasitic beings will often take advantage of you far more easily if your mind is altered.

It is open to debate as to whether it is safer to draw up your roots and shut the energy stream off after each session. I used to advocate always doing this but have since found that as long as one is protected and can regularly top up the energy then it is possible to be open for longer periods. Should you find your own energy levels depleting or that you are soaking up everyone else's 'stuff' then by all means visualise the energy going back down into the ground and draw up your roots. Should you find it easier to use the commonly activated 7 chakras instead then this also works well.

CHANTING

Prior to attempting to make direct contact via ritual there is another exercise you can practise. This is a chant. It will aid you into tapping into her energy and building up your own inner Lilith force. Chanting also helps us slip into altered states of consciousness essential for magical work. Used daily for several weeks it will continue to give access to her whenever you feel you need it. There is one found easily on the internet below but I found shortening it to only those aspects of her you wish to connect with works just as well. So, for example, you can use Lilith, Laylil, Lila and this chant will connect with the Jewish Lilith. Or Lilith, Lilitu, Ardat-lili can help if wishing to connect with her succubus aspect. And Lilith, Ninlil, Naamah helps with making contact with the younger Lilith. Lilith, Lamashtu, Lamia the vampire or hag Lilith. And so the permeations can go on. Repeat softly until you feel the air chill and

a subtle shift in energies.

The longer one some people use is, '*Lilith, Lilitu, Lamashtu, Lilu, Lamia, Lili, Lila, Lilit, Laylil, Ninlil, Lilyoth, Ardat-lili, Amezo, Makeda, Kali, Eilo, Lilith.*'

Hold that focus. Keep imagining a dark cave. Keep the focus on breathing. Nothing else. Eventually even this will fade and you should enter a trance state, here you stand the best chance of meeting Lilith.

If you enter the cave successfully you will be in a cold dark empty place. Here she waits. The only presence you should sense, is her. This is not the same as the dropping of the outer persona/ego shell and gnostic path, but is similar. Done often enough it can aid you in transforming on deep inner levels but only if you take both hers and your own advice. You are in charge. This is not a surrender, you have the choice at any time to say no to a suggestion.

The names I have given you are ones she is commonly known by, her Kali association is more on the energetic level than anything else. These are not all the same as the names given to the prophet Elijah but you could try using those as an alternative should you wish to. If so here they are.

Abeko, Abito. Amizo, Batna, Eilo, Ita, Izorpo, Kali, Kea, Kokos, Lilith, Odam, Partasah, Patrota, Podo, Satrina, Talto.

But she will also easily respond to a much shortened chant such as, *Lilith, Layil, Lili.*

2. *Protection* - Any system that doesn't include protection is potentially dangerous, not only do you need protection from spiritual entities who could harm or drain you but also as your awareness expands so your ability to recognise a psychic attack increases. In some respects we are often under them without consciously realising. Every time we annoy or irritate someone their negative thoughts or reactions are a form of psychic attack. And it is also

possible that at some point you could be under more serious threats from people so it is generally considered wise to protect yourself. This is a skill best well honed. It can save an awful lot of time and trouble if you are well covered, it's a sort of spiritual insurance plan.

I have three very simple rules regarding protection:

a. Use it daily
b. Vary it often
c. Tell no one what you use.

And with this in mind I shall refrain from giving examples of things to do as would give insight as to what I use. So my advice here is to read up on it, there are several good books on the subject and then expand your protection, be imaginative. It is always possible to accidentally call forth an unwanted entity or to underestimate one. Fae, for example can be tricksters and not always feel disposed to acquiesce to our requests. So having an insurance scheme is always of benefit and highly advised.

And if you should find yourself one day caught up in some sort of sordid magical war with another magician, have a backup plan. Yes ask Lilith for protection, it should be all you need unless She feels you could learn a valuable lesson by experiencing the full effects of it. If worried chose a deity, angel, spirit, ghost, demon etc. that no one would ever think of in relation to you, be obscure and ask said entity to completely shield itself from astral detection. As a final resort this normally does the trick.

3. *Ritual Construct* - If you are already trained or know a particular ritual format that works it should be easy to adapt it to Lilith. I don't personally believe that you need or have to perform rituals to connect with Lilith. Regular trance work will also have

the desired effect but rites are our opportunity to make offerings, give thanks and make pacts and requests. And this is welcomed and appreciated by most spiritual forces. I will suggest, however, that having a purpose to your rite is essential.

Lilith stems from ancient Middle Eastern pagan times as we know but as far as I know, apart from protection rites, there are no ancient invocation rituals to her for us to duplicate. Many have been created since these times and are out there in other books and on line for you to follow should you wish to. I am including several here for you to use.

But most importantly before conducting rites I was taught that one needs to prepare.

Here is a simplified list as general guidance for you to follow:

a. Just prior to your rite it is good to be able to bath in sea salt, it removes negative energies from your energy field. If not possible then a shower will have to suffice.

b. I advocate wearing comfortable clean loose fitting clothes/robes or go naked, which ever works best for you. Lilith has no set dress code. She does like hair to be loose and funnily enough for women she often inspires 'hairiness' generally.

c. Set up an altar facing north if possible, red altar cloth, one candle either red or black, a chalice of spring water, (to me this is essential as is conduit for spirit to enter and exit via) and an effigy or image of the Lilith you plan to call on (there are many though most people these days tend to get the Jewish Lilith or Naamah), snake skin, some cat fur or effigy of feline/lioness , owl feather and or effigy of owl. Plate for offerings, glass of wine, beer or red grape juice though she also likes pomegranate in my experience. And her sigil if you wish to use one. I don't care for over the top fussy altars. And most spirits prefer a clean and tidy environment.

On offerings, to me they operate on a sliding scale. If just a pile of fruit bought from a supermarket then she'll appreciate it but not as much as anything home made although it must be said she does love fruit whether bought or home grown! And let's put offerings and sacrifices in separate boxes here. To me a sacrifice is something of value that you are prepared to give up to her. The theory being among many traditions that more you value it the more a deity etc. will appreciate it. And as we know some cultures often held human sacrifice as the highest gift to their Gods. And much as I am sure that in some cases Lilith would love this, it goes without saying that legality of sacrifices is an issue here. In my experience we don't have to go to extremes. The more you give, or the more desperate you appear, the less you have to give in the future and the less you could be respected by Lilith. As for animal sacrifice, I have heard of some who have made such offerings to her and had them accepted and appreciated but could not comment on this myself as I have chosen not to.

How much time you are prepared to dedicate to the ritual is also a sacrifice of sorts as you are dedicating your time and energy to her. So if she knows you've sacrificed a night out or some other activity you enjoy for her ritual that is also appreciated. And again sacrifices also operate on a sliding scale, the more something means to you the more she will know you have been prepared to sacrifice.

On athames, staves, knives, wands etc . . . you can use them if you wish but they are not essential. Though charging up any magical tool with her energy is obviously a worthwhile thing to do as it is with most spirits. And as far as mixing energies is concerned, my view is that it is fine so long as they are part of the same family. For example, you could invoke Lilith and Samael together and imbue a wand with their force.

On personal blood offerings. – Most spiritual forces react positively to blood. Your own blood helps them to home in on you

and identify you from others. It is your life source. It links you to your ancestors so as long as you have made a pact with Lilith (or any spirit really) not to harm you or drain you in anyway then it should, in theory, be safe to offer your blood. But you don't need to be overly dramatic or leave permanent scars a few drops will suffice. There are some who would disagree here and say that you are risking allowing her to vampirize your life force this way, and in a way they are right, so it is absolutely essential to make a pact with her that she doesn't do this to you. When in doubt, leave it out.

Menstrual blood is more her preferred variety and can also be offered but usually in conjunction with specific rites, intents and desired results.

Offerings are usually made after invocation.

4. Make sure it is either sunset or night time. There is no need to stick to midnight but if you wish to then fine. Moon phases found best to call on most Liliths are dark moon, three days either side of full moon. Waning being the stronger for the most part.

5. On circle casting, some do this some don't. If you feel more protected and safer inside one then cast one by all means but some Lilith's might fail to turn up as they prefer to be unrestrained. To cover yourself from any harm her energy might do simply include a preparatory pact with her on first ever calling. Offer her incentive. As one of her children she is unlikely to wish you any harm but she will take initiates and those fairly new to her path on an inner journey of self recognition and bring up to the surface of your conscious mind all you have at your deepest depths. She will show you what you are truly capable of. Circle casting is more for keeping unwanted's out than protecting against any called within and as such some also take extra precautions by conducting a banishment of the space prior to ritual. I will leave such things up to your discretion.

But my own view is that if Lilith wants other spirits to take part then she knows best and if not she will banish them herself.

6. Opening yourself up energetically. This is to my mind the most important part of any rite, without being able to open up to spiritual energies/beings etc and being able to perceive them it all seems a little pointless. By invoking her you are allowing some of her energy to permeate you. It will literally flow through you, this is not possession, not even partial possession it is a basic level connection. What you are then shown once she arrives will be in your third eye or minds eye. And although all spiritual entities can manifest to a greater or lesser degree they rarely cross over fully into this plane. Now this doesn't rule out the potential for Lilith attempting a partial or full possession, but the latter should never ever be encouraged or attempted alone that is exceedingly dangerous. Partial ones are possible once you are further along your Lilith path and used to a great many of her forms and faces. Remember, she cannot over rule your free will. Full possessions minus concession are as rare as rocking horse poo and reserved for the realms of Hollywood. If you find her energy is getting too much simply ask her to ease off. It really is as simple as that. But that having been said going with a Lilith ride is usually one hell of a ride and well worth the journey.

If really concerned as to how to know if you are being possessed then should you begin to feel a massive thundering energy begin to charge at you and your central core begins to shake and wobble, if you feel as if you are losing control of your body or mind and that there is a sense of something far bigger than you trying to take over, then yes, it is possible you are experiencing an attempted possession. There will be extreme heat also. If so get someone to run you a cold bath and immerse yourself in it until all the heat and wobbling has gone.

7. The calling. Your candle is lit, you've opened up and now it is time to actually call her but what of those directions? Three are mentioned in Sumerian contexts. And some like to give each of the four major sacred prostitutes a direction each so calling them forth is popular among some Lilith devotees. The elements are found in many traditions so include them if you wish too.

I like to call the North as *'Lilith the Elder from whence we all come, upon which we all depend and unto which we will one day return.'* This can also be used for Earth.

East is traditionally the air element, *'The howling wind, the Lilitu, from the wilderness screech the scirlin and open the ways for Lilith'.*

South is the Sun and so are any of the names associated with her sons, e.g. Cain. *'The spirit of Cain the rising son the red one, the Witch Fire within, rise once more this hallowed night.'*

And lastly West is, *'Samael, Angel of Death, the guardian of the ghosts and dear departed ones, come forth oh consort of Lilith.'* These are a few simple suggestions. You can adapt and be inventive with your own also.

Sometimes I don't use any directions. Nor do I involve any invocation except Herself. And often this simplified rite can be the most powerful.

You can substitute the above for the names of the sacred prostitutes or the four Princes/Kings of Hell if used to working goetia or from grimoires.

THE INVOCATION

Each Lilith would have a slightly different format and calling however as emphasis of each one's energy varies. So I have listed below some examples of callings you can use for ones I am familiar

with. Any guidance regarding ritual structure that alters from the above suggestion is also included.

8.   The offerings, directly after the calling/conjuration the offerings or sacrifices are made in her name. And incense is lit, also in her name.

9. And now to sit patiently and go into your quiet meditative space, drift into the empty place of no-thing, the divide. She might have already arrived or you might have to wait. And the biggest question an uninitiated person asks is, 'How do I know when a spirit is with me?.' Here are some common signs that you have succeeded in evoking a spiritual being into your space.

Air pressure in your ears alters.

Air temperature either rises or drops noticeably.

Your candle with either burn longer or be blown out, Lilith prefers darkness.

You sense a presence as in that feeling of not being alone.

Your sigil, if there is one present, might give off a strange light or in one case once I saw smoke come from one made of clay.

You literally feel their energy all around you as a physical sensation. This is hard to describe and is one of those you have to feel it to know it situations.

Some of her energy will literally fill your body, this is physically tangible and impossible to deny as being very much for real.

Once their presence is detected it is usually easy to pick up on what sort of mood they are in and just like us this can vary.

Some people 'see' shadow, form and shape of deities, spirits etc. outwardly as well as inwardly, both in my mind are equally valid as representations of the being you have called upon.

If you have used the word 'invoke' then you can expect her energy to permeate you, often this is from feet upwards. This is in

no way as strong as a possession. Once filled with her energy it is easy for you both to communicate.

You might hear a voice, this is possible, but it is important to realise that you are hearing her from within, no matter how loud she may sound, the voice is an internal one. In my experience Lilith is not one to waste words, she is direct and succinct.

Images will be shown to you by spirits in your mind's eye. This is an easy way for them to communicate with us.

A particular mood will permeate you as will many inspirations and revelations.

And lastly out of ritual she will make her presence felt by popping up all over the place, expect massive co-incidences and seemingly incredible connections that have her stamp all over them. There will be signs, she might initiate ordeals, and omens a plenty, some to revel in and others to learn from.

10. Once she has arrived I find it best to let her direct which way the 'communion' part of the ritual goes. There are many ways. She might, if called in conjunction with Samael, inspire sexual energy from you. Whether you wish to allow this is up to you but don't be put off merely because you are alone, they are perfectly capable of taking you on that sort of journey should they wish to. But it is my opinion that sex magic or as is often termed sacred sex is best left for when you are more highly adept at working with Lilith and using your own Witchfire. My reason for saying this is that she is insatiable and loves to vampire sexual energy, so much like Asmodeus, she will gift you with an equally irrepressible sex drive. This is no blessing. Unless you have strong control then expect this to continue for anything up to nine months or so. It is also a strong lure but an easy route for those wishing to abuse their power and influence over you so be wary. It might be a more cerebral visit where important inspirations and messages pertinent to your

journey are conveyed. It could be purely energetic where she allows you to bathe in her energy and can sometimes cross into trance or partial possession, and as long as you still have full awareness this can be an amazing experience. There are many ways in which all the Liliths are able to commune with us. This is also your opportunity to make any pacts, declare your thanks for anything you feel she has bestowed upon you and to make any requests of her you feel you require her help with.

11. As you feel her energy start to drop or dissipate then it is time to say your goodbyes. This can be done by repeating the title you have given her during the invocation or calling followed by thanking her for visiting and bidding her farewell. And then is also time to say farewells to any directional spirits you might have also called upon. I find this order of basic communication works well for most invocations and most Liliths.
Invoke.
Give thanks and make offerings.
Commune (This can include pacts, requests etc.)
Give thanks again and farewells.

12. *Post Ritual* - This can vary from feeling ecstatic to melancholy. What ever the presiding mood of the rite there will be residual energy. Most people advocate grounding by eating some food. This often works well. But before any important revelations etc. are lost, write them down, recording your journey will ensure you don't lose or forget anything. If energy is still very high then going for a walk is also often a good idea.

13. *Patience* – If waiting for something you have petitioned or requested to occur don't expect instant results. They can happen but sometimes patience is required. She works in mysterious ways.

And once your connection is made she will know you. And I mean really know you, no thought or wish can be hidden from her, no fears or desires either. So don't go complaining if she manifests some of them. Lilith can be a journey of spiritual growth and wisdom if that is what you wish from her so tread cautiously and carefully, throw away wishes can also be quickly caught in her net and there is no good protesting that a week later you changed your mind. So always make absolutely sure anything you ask of her is what you truly want. And if needing extra guidance on this, use a form of divination prior to ritual to see if it is a wise move to progress with your petition.

And with this in mind the best form of divination where Lilith is concerned is to make a black mirror. This will become a scrying tool to aid you in both divining and also receiving images Lilith wishes to impart to you My modern version spares no apology for gaining it's inspiration from the 16th century *Munich Handbook of Necromancy* and the *Black Mirror of Munich*, the rites of which can easily be found on the internet. But as this was created in a time when occult work was closer in origin to Judaic and Christian Mysticism it puts some Lilith devotees off with some of it's content. That having been said if you can put your mind set in the head of a 16th century person without issue then it is a very powerful tool indeed, if not dangerous in some hands.

THE LILITH MIRROR & NECROMANCY

It is often said that Lilith resides in mirrors and therefore it is not the best of ideas to use a regular mirror to scry with. Instead you can make a black mirror for this. Simply acquire a piece of glass that you will be able to mount in a small frame that can be easily carried. Paint one side black. On this side in the centre paint in red or white Lilith's name in Hebrew לילית inside a six pointed star.

Below her paint Samael and his name in Hebrew as well סמואל. For him paint a serpent. To the left of Lilith paint Azazel עזאזל and lastly to the right Naamah נַעֲמָה.

On a dark moon charge yourself up and use your normal Lilith chant to partially invoke Lilith and when you feel the energies around you shift slightly it is a sign She has arrived.

Good places to use your mirror include, between graves in a graveyard, a cross roads, a liminal place such as beach, a cave or any desolate place that you feel drawn to. Once you have visited this place with your mirror and made offerings then this must be where you always return.

When ready take your mirror, a red rose (preferably acquired rather than bought), 6 copper coins, a bottle of beer or wine and some menstrual blood (if none available then sexual fluids are sufficient) to any of these places preferably at night and make offerings thus, "Some pennies for the dead I give" and throw them to the ground, it matters not where.

'*A drink for all to share I offer*', now empty contents on the ground.

'*This elixar of life I give*', and pour or offer cloth with fluid on to the ground also.

'*And this rose for Lilith maid is given*', and place it on the ground.

Then say, '*I summon you Lilith and your kin, in the name of Samael father of death, Azazel the strongest of spirits and Naamah daughter of fornication to come forth and show me your likenesses in this mirror when called and show me divine foresight on any matter I inquire upon*'.

Now return home by another route.

Each time you wish to use it to scry in take it back to the original spot you charged it in and summon them instructing them to appear

and show you what it is you wish to see.

The offerings only need doing the first time.

You can also summon spirits forth and use the mirror to see them in as an aid to necromancy communications.

(Based very loosely on the *Black Mirrors of Lilith* from the *Munich Necromantic Handbook*.)

OF STICKS AND STONES

Before going onto the ritual callings I felt it might help to include a brief list of some of the things she might inspire you to make, collect, charge and or use when working with her.

A poppet or doll to represent Lilith can be charged with her energy and placed as a central focal point to rituals and also used in more specific spell work made with her energy raised. A picture can also suffice. Any you create yourself will naturally be better received.

Wands and Lilith don't exactly have any traditional origin as such but if you feel her opposite number is Asherah this would work. She does resonate strongly with willow so it can be good to have something made of this wood that is used when calling on her. So whether it be wand or bowl, platter or talisman it doesn't really matter. If you are used to using a wand then don't be overly surprised if she inspires you to use it for less than traditional reasons.

Staves, staffs etc. are again not connected with Lilith but there's no harm in using them if you feel a rite calls for them.

A chalice or graal cup for water I consider essential as it provides a conduit for her to move through. Spring water being best. The material the vessel is made of doesn't seem quite so important.

A human skull. This has long been associated with Lilith, she connects strongest with the head and sexual organs. Also many who work with her are often inspired by her to also practise some

form of necromancy. Calling Lilith into a skull and then keeping this purely for her is a traditional Lilith/Witch practise. Naturally a real one is preferable and can be obtained in many countries perfectly legally as often sold for medical purposes. But an artificial one can also suffice. My suggestion though would be to craft one yourself from clay or wood as she is not a fan of plastics. You can decorate it with her sigil.

Athame / Sword not required as such but a blade sharp enough to pierce skin to make blood offerings with is required. This can also be achieved with sterile needles.

Owl feathers, wings, etc. the middle eastern screech owl is associated with Lilith but I also feel that the eagle owl is probably more her bird.

Anything rotting or decaying whether of flesh and blood or plant life appeals to her.

Dregs of wine, save the dregs from bottles and then decant so you always have some to offer her.

Snake skin, unless you have a live one as a pet who might oblige you in a ritual (baring in mind it's environmental requirements might not mix).

Some say that a feline element is needed and as many who have cats know they are frequent visitors to rituals.

If working with Lilith in a sexual context you could find that she likes to bring sex toys into things. But not tacky plastic battery operated ones. Any made of more natural substances such as metal, glass, wood, leather work well with Lilith. Anything that inflicts physical pain.

SIGILS

Symbols and sigils related to individual spirits, and occasionally combined ones, are traditionally used in ritual mostly as a way of

ensuring the correct entity is invoked and can then also be charged up with the energy of said spirit for future use. The sigil itself contains part of said entity. By creating our own ones we are able to use unique tools but you can also buy ready made varieties. The sigils have the ability to help direct power in specific directions. This is not in any way the same as sigil craft, which is different. There you create a simple one line sentence, carefully crafted excluding negatives and being ultra cautious about your wording, be careful what you wish for etc. and then reduce this sentence by removing the vowels and repeated letters until you have a string of letters. These can then be made into a symbol/sigil to represent your intent. The sigil is used by various methods to force your will upon the universe in a manner that requires you to see the effect already manifesting.

So as you can see using specific sigils in ritual is more about identification. It adds power to your calling/invocation. It is not absolutely necessary to use sigils and also tends to differ in level of importance depending on your path/tradition. Those working goetia nearly always use sigils. You might well have found that your first introduction to a spirit is by them revealing their sigil to you. This in itself is useful in identifying what or who exactly has made contact whether it is through meditation, visualisation, and or magical ritual. It isn't always an assurance some spirits are tricksters and play devious games but wasting time on identification can be counter productive sometimes. The best gauge often is to retrace your steps. As in, 'how did I reach this point?', 'What was the purpose to my meditation etc?,' 'what else have I been working with of late, are there any links?' and, 'what am I hoping to attract in my life?', these examples of questions to ask yourself will aid you best in homing in on what you are picking up on. Also going by your own intuition and how the spirit makes you feel is a very good way of knowing if it is likely to be of benefit to you or not.

Having said all this, here are some commonly accepted sigils for some of the spirits mentioned in this book.

Lilith

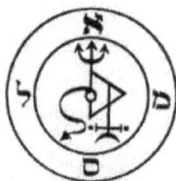 

Samael

Azazel

Asmodeus   Lucifer

SHAPE SHIFTING

Most witches/shamans will come across the practise of shape shifting at some point. There are those who claim that a literal physical transformation takes place whilst others say not so, it is an advanced but ancient form of astral travel tha can project beyond the veil into reality. My only experience is with the latter, I cannot advise on the literal form. So no, I cannot teach you how to grow extra limbs and wings and things, but you will find that by focusing in on a creature associated with the spirit you are working with you can eventually, if said spirit goes along with it, be able to take on it's form on astral planes. This will enable you to hide your own identity to a degree and give access to the mind set and instincts and wisdom of the one you are shifting into alliance with. So begin by simple meditations. With Lilith is is most likely to be snake but might also be owl or cat. Birds are one of the most commonly popular creatures to shift into as the concept of flight in our minds embraces the idea of liberty and freedom of restrictions.

Shape shifting can be used as a direct way of gaining information, working magic elsewhere etc. the ideas are as limited as your imagination. Taking your meditation to the next level, that of trance, should enable you to adjust your mind set to that of the creature you wish to shift into. Giving as much time as possible to learning everything about each one will help but you really have to try and imagine what it might feel like to be that creature. And don't limit yourself to the physical feeling, go by the smell of it, how it might see, hear, taste etc. The more you indulge your own senses and psyche in that of the one you wish to shift into the easier it will be. And if unsure of success find a trusted friend. Offer to visit them. See if they pick up on your presence. Shape shifting gives you an alternative view of life. It allows you access to slightly different astral realms.

Spell Craft

There are, as we know, many spells to protect people from Lilith but what about using Lilith to aid you in casting spells? Well naturally this can work. Writing down an intent, using sigils, or herbs, incense, charms, amulets, talismans etc. can all be charged with Lilith's energy during ritual and give an added turbo to your magic. Just make sure with any such thing that you truly, really do want the outcome. An adept magician/witch should reach a point where spells are rarely utilised or needed, their mere thoughts become the magic. Until you reach this point, if indeed you do, then by all means ask Lilith or any of her kin to aid you in your casting of spells. One way of testing how far you have got is to write down a simple petition on paper or parchment, hold it between your hands, open up and channel earth energy then chant *Lilith, Laylil, Lili* and feel the earth energy being driven into the spell. Once you sense the air shift around you then if it is a physical manifestation you require bury the spell and wait. If purging or banishing, burn it. If cleansing and healing, cast it into water, and if a desired communication or inspiration rip it into pieces and cast it to the wind.

On Requests

You might be one of the few she grants all wishes to. I wouldn't personally see this as a good thing. Sometimes we are given enough rope to hang ourselves with. So, be really careful and specific in your wishes. Protection is one of her major strengths, so this is always worthwhile asking for. And she will happily take you inwards on a voyage of self-discovery and insight leading to mystical knowledge. She can open doors to the dead, or at least by working with her you will find it easier to do any mediumistic work or necromancy. And as for our cultural or personal morals and ethics, forget it,

she doesn't have them. Money doesn't seem to interest or concern her, so asking for riches rarely works, not directly at least. Sexual partners will nearly always be granted. Inspiration creatively also. Any career involving death, the dying, detective work, solitary isolation, she frequently gives strength to but she is an outlaw so criminal activities are often her domain as well. Invisibility is often granted. As is any occult or esoteric pursuit. Her world is often seedy, a counter cultured underworld. Here you find most forms of Lilith. Or a place of total solitude. All these things are helpful to tune into and be mindful of when requesting things of her. If wishing to become a lawyer or union rep etc. she's always up for a battle of minds. Mind games do appeal to her, but only if there is gain to be had from it. Lilith has an almost exhaustible and excessive insatiable energy, it knows no bounds, it has none. And as such any addictive aspects of your personality could be exploited. So again be wary what you wish for.

Sex in Ritual

Those familiar with combining sexual energy in rites are unlikely to be at all fazed by this but for those who are already feeling awkward here are my views on the subject. Prior to encountering it for the first time it does indeed seem odd and is often seen as, or the province of, people wishing to use the magical realms and world as a means by which to gain more sexual partners. And the occult world past and present has many such people. So I feel it is important to know why you wish to do it and, what is more, are comfortable with the idea before opening up on this level. As there is a strong link between Lilith in most of her forms and sex it makes sense that she inspires it in us during ritual sometimes.

This having been said not everyone who works with Lilith raises any sexual energy in rituals to her. It might all come down

to preference, pacts, inspiration and what you hope to achieve. It is unlikely that you will conduct Lilith rites and not have sexual energy activated at some point whilst on your journey with her however. It is very important, in my view, to have this as an option rather than an absolute. So some of the rituals listed out below have sex as an option in varying degrees of importance. What you decide to do is entirely up to you. And unless deliberately invoking Lilith and inviting partial or full possession then you should always have full control of yourself. The latter being inadvisable unless in the company of those familiar with such an act who can protect you.

There are many ways and reasons for combining sexual energy with Lilith work. It does indeed bring you closer to her and allow for her to develop a deeper and stronger connection with you. This, to me, is the best reason. In opening up sexually with her, and I do mean *with* her, you are touching a core essence of Lilith. This is on a primal level and intensely powerful. It doesn't seem to bother Lilith if you have a partner to share this with or not, in fact if the partner is reticent or not up to Lilith's energy sexually she can flip into hag quite easily and be put off. And this will and can affect relationships. It takes a feisty, strong person to ride Lilith from either perspective. Anyone not up to the job will lessen in interest to her and vice versa. So there is a lot to be said for keeping this as a solitary practice.

But, this having been said there are some couples that can and do work with Lilith together very successfully. And many a coven that manages to also.

Sex in ritual is nothing new. There is evidence for it in many ancient cultures especially in the pre-Judaic Middle East. But it is not something to open up to without feeling completely comfortable about it. And it will always vary. You might wish to invoke Lilith and Samael in a tantric session. It could be a deliberate act of sex magic you wish to conjure up. Or maybe even a taboo subject such as necromantic sex. But whatever the reason she will nearly always

reply to both sexual energy and blood and she will happily drain you of both if you are weak.

So there is a lot to be said for keeping this as a solitary practice. And for those of you wondering if this requires a woman calling upon her to be bi-sexual or gay then no, not at all. It is your sexual energy that she will home in on. She will however tap into what is inspiring you and find this as a key signature from then on. It probably sounds perverse or peculiar to many to imagine allowing yourself to take such a journey alone but once you get used to it, like any practise, it become second nature. You might well find it is Samael, Azazel, Asmodeus or sometimes Lucifer who come forth in Lilith rites where sexual energy is raised.

Other reasons and purposes include standard sex magic aiming for a specific result. Or tantric sex, as in with-holding orgasm and raising kundalini energy for a specific magical purpose is a popular reason for doing it. It can be used to gain access to ecstatic trance and otherworldly experiences although sex is not needed as such to achieve this as we know.

But, it is not essential to include any sexual energy in rituals to Lilith. Or any spiritual being for that matter. If it goes against the grain or you are really put off by it then she might well encourage you to look deeply into why you are uncomfortable with the idea but she won't ever force you or reject you over it. In fact holding back from giving her what she wants is often a good thing, and is frequently respected.

She is, after all, one of our most well-known icons for sexual independence and that includes the right to say no, she did!!

The Ritual Callings

Lilitu the Wild One
(Akkadian Storm Demons)

Other ways of deepening the connection with primal Lilith are to spend several days and nights out in a wilderness alone. Though possibly a risky venture, it is extremely effective at touching the wilder aspect of her nature. Simply use the names I have chosen above as a chant to call her. If you were successful the first time then you should be able to re-connect without any real problems.

Firstly it is probably a good idea to ask yourself why you wish to call upon this potentially destructive force. If you find you have a good reason for it and no other will do then fine, go ahead by all means. Some of you might wish to invoke sudden dramatic changes in your lives. Lilitu will do this for you so be fairly specific about what kind of changes you are after and keep in mind these will be stormy ones not easy ones.

You can, should you desire it, stir up a storm in the lives of others. For some this would extend beyond their spiritual ethical boundaries but for those who don't worry about such things then invoking her for black magic purposes is possible.

But as with any new spiritual entity you call on I advise meditating on them and your purpose for calling first. In this case take what you know of her and in your imagination reduce it to the purest thought form energy you can manage. Then simply allow images to flow into your mind's eye. Feel the energy, smell it, hear it, taste it, smell it and imbue it. Record your findings in any way that works for you. If possible do several of these prior to your planned event. There are intelligences to all spirits but personally I find linking with the pure energetic form helps to make sure I can identify them

in the future. Spirits, as we know, can wear masks and take multiple forms and again, Lilith is no exception.

Those familiar with regular rituals will know that forward planning if sometimes employed before a rite but also spontaneous ones can have great effects also. As a very general guide the new moon is a good time to connect with any chaotic forces. The energies of a new moon have open ended possibilities. Unpredictable yes, but then that is what you are after. Decide on a time and place. Make sure this is possible. She is a nocturnal energy so the time would have to be after sunset. She is a swirling vortex of force so I feel that any form of spiral or dervish style dance would be fantastic to use to aid invocation. This is just my opinion however you may disagree or see differently. This form of Lilith is very early and unsophisticated, it is raw, primal, and will be more drawn to your own inner primal force. By opening up your deepest core to her you can attain a strong degree of connection without the need for elaborate words. A standard circle casting is unlikely to have any effect on this Lilith. So wafting a besom about is not really going to cut it. As your intention is to stir up a primal force of nature then hot fiery incenses work well. Things such as Cayenne pepper, sandalwood, dragon's blood, arrow root, poppy seeds and the like are good.

The only similar force I can liken this one to that many of you might already be familiar with her in the West is The Morrigan.

Items and the like you might want to include:

~The only animal totem linked with this Lilith is the Anzu bird. So any effigies or representations of eagle owls or feathers of such a bird would work well as things to incorporate into your ritual. Sand to sprinkle on the floor.

~A bowl of water.

~A Black and Red candle.

If wishing to keep things simple this is all that is required.

So here is my Lilitu Storm Demon Rite:

New Moon Night.

Sprinkle sand on the floor.

Have bowl of water nearby for vortex to come through from.

Open up energy centres or charge up energetically, amplify your witch fire in whatever way you usually do it.

This first part of the rite is conducted in as dark a room as you can make it or outside on a dark moon night.

Either dance around the bowl imagining a storm as you do, you are conjuring the storm by dancing. Or if wishing to go for a spinning dervish style, then to the side of the bowl.

Once weary of dancing sit and chant; '*Lilitu, Ardat-lili, Laylil, Lilith*' keep chanting until you feel your root or serpent tail twitch and energy around you shift.

Light candles and incense and say: '*Lilitu be welcome, Lilitu be here, Lilitu demon of night storms, terror of the skies, dreaded of the ancients, she whose presence strikes pure fear into mortal souls, she whose energy raises women and children into the air, she who comes from space of no space, whose place is no place, whose face is wrought on destruction, be here this dark moon night but protect me and those I love from any harm your energy could cause.*'

Sprinkle more incense.

'*Lilitu origin of Lilith whose beginnings are lost in our memories, whose source is before the Gods, who came first and stirred up the storms that charged the air and gave life to earth, mother of lightning of wind of change initiate this in my life* (or substitute this for whoever else you are wishing Her energy upon) *let that which was set and stuck as is be forced to break and buckle under your breathe. Come like a howling from the West and warn only briefly*

of your arrival, before you strike with your strength. *Clench your talons into my flesh* (or the one you are wishing this upon) *and accept this small offering of blood.'* Make offering, remember only a few drops.

Next are words to use of wishing Lilitu upon another.

'*Take the spirit of up into the air, turn their world upside down, shake them to the core, let them feel your energy permeate their life for a short while and then drop them back down to earth.'*

If calling on her for your self say next:

'*Take my spirit up into the air, let me find my wings and learn to fly with you and rise above all petty mortal issues. Allow me to accept the need for sudden major change in my life and the ability to see the bigger picture as you do.'*

Now sit quietly and if she hasn't already totally arrived await her presence.

Make offerings, this Lilitu will want more blood so a fresh heart procured from a butchers is a good idea. To be left outside or taken to your nearest wild or desolate place after the rite. If you haven't such a thing to hand then more of your own will keep her happy.

Give thanks.
Commune.
Close.
Ground.

ARDAT-LILI

Now some see Ardat-lili as pretty much the same as the storm demon Lilitu but to me she has the added quality of succubus and it is this aspect of her nature we can call upon with a specific invocation. Bear in mind with Ardat-lili that calling her can bring the hag through as well so you could begin by invoking the sexier seductress and end up with the hag.

Invoking a succubus can be fun but it can also draw someone to you so unless you want that attention then be careful with this one. She often enchants men to fall for specific women. This can seem as strong as falling in love but is usually infatuation. Once her interest wanes so does the magic. She is more likely to inspire him to be promiscuous, and free spirited sexually or bring his repressions to the surface. A succubus can also distract a man and be a means of sapping some of his energy. For a woman she increases lust and dreams of lovers. She can also aid you in revealing which men lust after you, if any that is. If called upon to pep up an ailing relationship she can ignite sexual desire in a man but he might not wish to share this with his partner so be aware that it could back fire in this way. And don't complain if he is sneaking off to see women of the night.

All this having been said should you still wish to invoke her then here is one method:

Lay a large red cloth upon your bed or floor. Light one red candle near your window. Use a musk based incense. Prepare as per normal. No altar is required. Place items you associate with sex upon your cloth. Be naked. Anoint yourself sparingly with musk, rose or patchouli oil on third eye, breast, naval, outside of sexual organs. She likes pungent flowers such as white Lilies. Food wise she only wants sexual energy so unless you are prepared to give her this then don't bother calling on her. This is not an initiate's rite. If calling her with a partner then it is often a good idea to try something new sexually to attract her. Your normal sexual practises might not gain her attention. Ask each other for any hidden fantasies and be brave in allowing any you are prepared to experiment with as a lure to help gain her attention. If solitary then indulge in visual fantasies until all are played out. When ready begin chanting whilst having sex, '*Lilitu, Ardat-lili, Laylil, Lilith*' until your third eye begins to buzz and you sense a shift in energies around you. Hold back from orgasm and take a temporary break fro m sexual activity whilst you

turn your attention to calling on her.

Open up energetically and magically.

If in a couple or group situation have one person elected as the invoker say, *'Ardatlili mistress of the night, the primordial serpent, she who brings carnal lusts into our minds and our bodies, harlot, whore, and holy virgin, she who cannot have sex as a woman can, she who cannot bare children as women can, the frustrated bride, she who is drawn to our sexual energy and inspires our men to be passive in her presence, domina, Queen of temptations, cross the abyss, rise up through the void, enter this domain, share with us your sexual energy, but protect us from your insatiable side let us be sated by your presence.'* whilst your partner or the rest of the group participants hold a mildly sexual light trance.

Then wait, until you feel her arrive and when she does let her join with you sexually offering up your orgasm in her name. This can be most effective if used in sex magic. So adding an extra line such as, *'As we offer you our orgasm and creative force we petition you to make manifest our desires.'* making sure you both or all think of exactly the same thing at the same time and are able to synchronise orgasms, this being easiest if solitary as no synchronicity is required and hardest for a group to ever manage.

Speak – *'Oh Ardat-lili mistress of the night, she who sneaks into the beds of men, keeper of the secret desires, sharer of the dreams of men, she who arouses them to great heights and fulfils all their carnal wishes, the primal seductress, succubae, wily woman, harlot, whore, and virgin, come this night, fly here to this space I have prepared for you, be privy to my mind and its wishes, see the images I wish to make manifest, protect me from any harm these might do but let them flow out into the night to land upon those I wish you to influence. Accept this incense, take my orgasm and imaginings as my gift to you.'*

Most callings to Ardat-lili are solitary. It is slightly rarer for a

couple to call on her and invoke a succubus unless they wish to extend their sex life and include more people. There is naturally an ethical element here, not everyone wants a succubus visiting to inspire them into group sex.

Once the congress has finished then sit in meditative state for a while in case she has any visuals she wishes to impart to you.

Give thanks and close.

Nin-lil

Lilith and Samael were torn apart, he sent 'down' to roam the earth and become The Satan as well as retaining his title as Angel of Death, she flees Adams attempts at seduction/rape to the Red Sea and is free to do as she pleases including inspiring the seduction of Eve and fall of humankind.

Ninlil's mythos is similar, her lover is cast out and sent down into the underworld, she follows him and they create two Gods of this world, and two above. Theirs starts with a heavy handed seduction/rape but ends as a love story.

Altar facing North.
Cloth White or dark blue.
Candle Black.
Water.
Incense, light fragrant perfumes.
Offerings - Flowers, beer, seeds of grain, flax, loaves.

You can use the basic ritual construct at the beginning of the chapter for calling on Ninlil.

Invocation

'Beloved Ninlil, wife of Enlil the unclean and deported one, mother

of Naana the Moon God. She who bathes in the waters of Nippur whose song inspires such lust as cause's men to lose their minds and forget their manners. She who rebels against her mother's advice she who knows her own mind. Oh beautiful one of the night, lady of the moonlit air, she who follows Enlil and no matter his disguise is wise to his deceptions. She who is his love and he hers come this night and share with me safely some of your energy.'

Light incense.

'Wise lady of the night, the gentle one, whose persistence and determination bares fruit in spite of seemingly overwhelming odds, come and fill me with your sense of purpose, your strength and stamina and fearless abandon. Imbue me with the ability to break free from any over protective chains that seek to bind me and allow me freedom to make my own mistakes enabling me to learn and grow with new vigour. Accept here these offerings of beer, grain, bread and flowers and this incense burned in your honour.'

Wait for her to arrive.

Give thanks.

Top up incense.

Commune.

Close.

NAAMAH

To me Naamah is a more sophisticated version of Ardat-lili and therefore another succubus and a sacred prostitute. Naamah is perfect to call on for any form of sex magic. Her energy should give an added boost to your workings if they are of this nature. In Hebrew her name means "pleasant." But there are several Naamahs. The one linked closest to Lilith is the demonic one.

Naamah is not, like her predecessor, going to transform into a hag at any point. She is all maid. This being is youthful and sexual. She is beauty and attractiveness. She might represent outer aesthetics

Naamah by Gillian Macdonald

but to know Naamah you have to be prepared to delve under her skin. Her energy is addictive, it is rarely sated and is undeniably intoxicating. Allowing yourself to fall under Naamah's spell could lead you into an addictive place where an obsession with looks, both yours and your attractions, will rule many of your decisions and directions in sexual partners. This essentially superficial world does indeed have a tougher interior but piercing Naamah's heart is not easy. She is fickle, flighty, and childlike. She challenges your relationship with youth and vitality. As we already know her mythos in the Zohar tells of her working with Lilith to corrupt Adam during his wilderness years and mating with him to create plagues cast upon mankind. She is also a consort of both Samael and Asmodeus. She delights in splitting up couples and causing mayhem in relationships. She is also held responsible for epilepsy in children. So if you plan to work with her as a couple it needs baring in mind that she might test your relationship. Calling upon her with either Samael or Asmodeus is a good idea as it balances out her energy and gives her a consort so lessening any possible mischief.

Best moon phase New.

Direction North.

Candles Red x 2.

Flowers White lilies.

Incense Rose oil, acacia resin, Greek rose, jasmine oil.

Offerings Fruit as in apples or pomegranates, nuts, berries, sweet meats.

Wine or flowery cordial.

Fetish - poppet or image.

Bowl or chalice of water.

Snake skin.

Cloth Red.

Time after sun down.

Prepare yourselves as you normally would.

Open up energetically and bring up as much serpent energy as

possible this should be a kundalini experience.

Light both candles and incense.

One chants, '*Naamah Lilith Naamah.*'

Whilst the other says:

'*I call upon Naamah the beautiful one, she who is most pleasing to the eyes, lady of fornication who arrives by night, mistress of my dreams, she who intoxicates me and fills me with divine pleasure. I/we wish our skin to tingle with your touch, to feel you as you rise up inside us filling us with divine bliss, oh wise and cunning Naamah she who can put angels under her spell, she whose lust knows no bounds, whose perfume is the sweetest known to man, whose consort is (Samael or Asmodeus) and whose mother is Lilith, come this night accept our offerings of flowers, incense food and wine.*'

Now sit and both quietly visualise Naamah with her consort making lustful love.

Samael invocation:

'*I call upon Arch Angel Samael, Angel of Death of the sphere of Hod, the desolation, Prince of the Fifth Heaven bringer of War. He who is Gods wrath and heralds its arrival on this earthly plain. Samael reaper of souls, he who tempted Eve and fathered Cain but had his Lilith torn from him and was castrated and now blinds us with light as his brilliance casts illusions in our minds. Samael the dark one whose serpentine energy rises up and calls his Lilith to return whilst she makes sport with sleeping mortal men. He of the shadows, the Satan sent to tempt us into going against our own better judgement, he who was cast down to entice us into liberating ourselves from dogma and indoctrination. In the name of El Elohim I invoke thee to be here in this space created for you and ask you to protect me and my kin from any harm your energy might cause me whilst in my presence.*'

Or if you prefer:

Asmodeus Invocation

'I/we call upon Asmodeus King of Demons, Prince of seven Hells. Demon of lust and wrath, he who loved Sarah and was summoned to aid Solomon in building his temple. Asmodeus whose energy is fire, whose month is November, the Devil on Two Sticks, he who hides his feet from men. Asmodeus the lawyer, governer and trickster, he who is red of skin, take this Naamah daughter of Lilith let her sate your lust and calm your wrath, take this one as your consort this night in our presence but protect us from any harm your energy could cause us. Make sport with her, mix your energies together and allow us to bathe in them and be strengthened by them after we offer you these gifts in your name. We summon thee up from the abyss this night.

(And are prepared to make a pact with you to this effect), we summon thee from the abyss here this night.'

The latter only needed to make the first time unless you wish to negotiate a deal with him, he is not that easy to haggle with however. Some find him indifferent to a woman's call unless she is of exceptional interest to him. His wrath is fast and furious.

He hates water so cover the chalice at this point and make offerings to him as it is easy for him to possess and drain people of energy it is best not to offer him blood. Often sexual energy will suffice as will sharing the offerings you already have made to Naamah. Also avoid fish and feathers or birds with Asmodeus, they will put him off.

Make your offerings stating that you wish for them to be accepted in their names.

Before congress make sure you both watch out for each other, boundary lines need setting prior to his arrival, have safe words or signals if frightened, and insist he desists if too much or becoming dangerous. He does respect things like this as a rule.

Be extremely thoughtful over any deals made.

Personally I'd always rather stick to Samael with Naamah, his energy is more predictable and somewhat safer. Asmodeus can be too intense and over powering often seeping into your everyday life and affecting your own aura and those of people around you. Also if prone to rage or anger he is definitely best avoided unless you plan to use this deliberately. This doesn't mean to say you can't work with him just that out of the two Samael came first and the Asmodeus link is a later one. Those already familiar with goetia shouldn't have too many problems with him however.

If able to re-balance then allow some time to ask for his assistance in any way.

Close when ready to.

JEWISH LILITH

This is the Lilith most are familiar with and a direct link to the hag or crone aspect of Lilith. You could get both. This is the Lilith of wasteland and places between worlds. Anywhere liminal or melancholic will suit this Lilith as a place to call on her but she is equally at home in your home. Cellars, caves, unused rooms can appeal to her and aid in creating the atmosphere she is drawn to. You could set aside a space permanently for her and I'm sure she will appreciate it but you can just as easily be more flexible especially if short of space.

Direction North.

One candle, if that, some find total darkness works best.

An earthy, incense.

6 red roses.

Wine or port, dregs of

Pomegranate.

Snake skin.

Owl feathers.

Image or poppet of her.

Water.

Put down your roots and draw up energy from below. Start the chant, 'Lilith, Laylil, Lili' and keep this going. Feel the energy rise and hold it in your tail bone. You can allow it to arouse you, should that be your intent, or not as the case maybe. Refrain from letting the sexual energy from getting too strong, control it and let it rise up through your spine whilst gently rocking back and forth. Once you reach your third eye keep it flowing from below to this point, if raising Kundalini energy is your goal this should work if practised frequently enough. If you have decided just to raise her energy minus the sexual aspect that can continue out through your crown.

Now say your invocation by repeating the following words out loud.

Chant *'Lilith, Laylil, Lili'* until you feel energies shifting.

Light candle.

Invocation.

'I call upon Lilith, Queen of the Night, Mother of demons, consort of Samael, mother of Azazel and Naamah.

She who comes forth by night to bring either temptation or terror to man.

She who resides in shadows and desolate places.

The screech owl, the serpent, first born.

She who rejected Adam and fled.

She who liberates.

The first rebel.

She who pushes against convention and drives pleasure from pain.

The night hag.

Who creeps up on her prey through the door of allure and seduction.

She who creates and destroys.

She most feared.
The ancient one Lilith.'
Light incense in her honour.
Make offerings.
Visualise Lilith and Samael in congress and allow them to reveal their energy to you.
Ask for them to share their energy with you but to protect you from any harm it might do.
Give thanks.
Make petitions.
Meditate and ask for guidance.
(Possible congress.)
Close.

LUCIFER

If wishing to call upon this angelic force it helps to understand a little of the nature of this energy. He/she is not some red skinned horned creature, far from it, there is nothing 'devilish' about Lucifer. Lucifer is light, the inner light, the light that is first and last each day. If you do see him/her in a human like form they are often fair haired and pale skinned. But this can vary. This is light that leads to revelations, illuminations and greater understanding. It is intensely powerful, only the tiniest micro-fraction of angelic energy can usually be tolerated by us mere mortals. And even this is over powering at times. Lucifer can feel suffocating at times. But, he/she is a good balance to Lilith's energy so is very worth calling upon if only for this reason alone.

Use your Jewish Lilith altar but before invoking her call upon Lucifer. Adding Lucifer's sigil to the altar will help. Add a yellow candle to it also.

If you can bare the smell, Lucifer likes sulphur. A tiny amount burned on charcoal will suffice. Once he/she is invoked you can add

your usual Lilith incense.

'Lucifer, Lumière, Venus, star of the morning, star of the night, he who was first born light of our days who fell and anchored deep in the earth, whose presence burns below us and above us, who is the illuminated one, Phosphorous the light bringer, the angel of Love, lust and rebellion. I call upon you asking you to protect me from any potential harm your energy might cause me and bring balance and harmony to Liliths energy here this night/morning. Accept my offerings of incense, wine and fruit, given to both you and Lilith with love and respect.'

Then call on Lilith.

The shared energies will feel different than when you call on Lilith alone. Any matters relating to giving inner strength, new light on old problems, love issues, wisdom of a higher nature, new ideas creatively, protection from any who wish you ill or harm etc. can now be made.

Commune.

Close.

NIGHT HAG

Meeting the crone aspect of Lilith can for some be a terrifying experience. Frequently she will delight in appearing to men after first luring them into her cave with her more youthful face and figure. I've found that women tend to meet her in a less sexual context and more often than not when they require some increased inner strength and resilience. But this can vary. Deliberately invoking this most melancholic of all Lilith's is not always easy. She is the most 'no nonsense' Lilith and the one least likely to bother with anyone whom she views as a time waster or player in spiritual arts. This Lilith is often blunt and harsh in her response. Her voice is deep and gravelly her energy dark, cold and intense. She is closest of all Lilith's to the underworld and the best one to invoke if wishing to

work in a mediumistic manner or if needing help in most forms of necromancy. I've met this Lilith on many occasions. My pact or deal with her was to finish this book and she will finally aid me in coming out the other side of a prolonged menopause. If, like myself, you are a woman of a certain age wishing to 'crone' this is the Lilith for you. As with many popular views on crones she represents the cumulative experience and knowledge of all Lilith's.

INVOCATION

Time - Dead of night.

Moon phase - It doesn't really seem to matter.

Indoors or outdoors but as dark as possible.

If you use any incense before plunging yourself into the dark, make it of a musty earthy variety, and include some ground bone powder or the ashes of a dead soul (animal or human).

Items of use - Skull to charge with her energy.

Earth from a graveyard or actual grave if calling on a specific soul.

Dead or decaying items generally.

Any direction will do.

CALLING

'I call upon Lilith, the Nighthag, the crone, she who only ever comes by night, she of the underworld, she who chooses to live with the dead and prey on the living.

Oh most terrifying of hags, she whose face sends fear into the souls of men, she who laughs at our troubles, she who works with Ardat - lili and preys upon men whilst they sleep, invoking wet dreams and appearing to them as they spill their seed.

She who is the wisest and most intelligent of all Liliths, the brain, the one closest to death.

Protect me from any harm that you or any spirits drawn to me may attempt to cast upon me.

Grandmother of life, she whose mysteries run deepest of all, the melancholic one who is more at home with the souls of the dead than the living.

Come to me this dark night.

Accept my offerings.

Share with me some small insight into your ways and how they may best aid me.

Accept my petition/s and grant them.' (Petition)

Communion.

Give thanks.

Close.

EPILOGUE

The Lilith I work with is from a pre-historic past. She was here when polytheistic pagan traditions were the norm. She was here before them. She acknowledges all spiritual entities. Her main colour is red, it is of blood and she is scarlet for a reason. She is able to use the chord of blood that ties us to the spirit world. Through our life force she can connect with each of us. She is in our blood, some more so than others. She is the blood of menstruation, the waste blood, the blood that the grail rejects. She is the Whore of Babylon, the force that both lead to its creation and its fall, here before us and hence the mother of creation. To have a consort who is death makes perfect sense.

Lilith women, and I use this term loosely, are not normally dutiful wives and mothers. If they try and fit this socially acceptable archetype it can be like going against their natural grain. A woman with a strong Lilith spirit will be restless and unsettled in a marriage, and can make for a terrible mother. There are naturally

exceptions but aspects of this are often the norm. And in ancient times it was how Lilith women were identified. Those who were barren, or unfaithful, or chose prostitution frequently fell into the Lilith camp. Those of wealth who could afford to lead promiscuous lives and get away with it by indulging their free spirited whims would be tarnished to a degree but their status often saved them from reprisals. And the very worst Lilith women, in most cultures, were the witches, those who worked secret spells by moon night and called upon the demonic realms and creatures of the night, they were the most feared. Many go their entire lives not really understanding or acknowledging that it is indeed Lilith motivating, inspiring and moving their spirits so. The role of whore or adulterer also appealed to Lilith women so some became mistresses. And all of this is still happening to this day. None of this has changed. But what has occurred that appeals to Lilith women is sexual freedom, equal working rights and the improved liberation that much of the Western world offers her.

That Lilith is so prevalent in modern contemporary literature is no accident. She is a muse. She loves words. She uses them as wisely and intelligently as a high ranking Queen's Counsel does. This modern Lilith is celebrated by many, especially feminists. Indeed there is even a feminist magazine with her name. She has become an icon for independent self-reliant women who seek equality with men on all levels. She knows the only real difference between us is in our reproductive roles. Feminists see her as the liberated feminine. She is likely to be one who can survive with or without a man in her life regardless of her sexual preferences. She will often deliberately take on jobs formerly seen as men's roles in life. Feminist Lilith's can be found in the military, emergency services, politics, law, builders, tree surgeons the list could go on for some time here. A feminist Lilith feels she has something to prove to herself and others. She often has way more testosterone flowing through her than many

women do and as such her sex drive can be insatiable. As this child of Lilith matures she will often slow down a bit. These Lilith women can often burn themselves out at a young age. But it is their nature to do so. And here in the Western World especially she has an outlet. Here she can be this woman. She is not expected to marry or have children, she can choose how her life will pan out.

And if she chooses to be a sexually free spirit and not ever be pinned down to a monogamist relationship then she can do this without fear or reproach from any religious laws. Lilith has come into her own in many modern societies.

But she can also be the mother. It is possible for Lilith women to have children, they might not be the best of mothers or they could be the most over protective variety. But something about them will set them apart from most mums. She will respond to a woman's open or secret wishes not to have children. So if a woman wants a miscarriage, Lilith will oblige her, if she is to be such a terrible mother that she wishes someone else would take her children away then Lilith will deal with this also. So they might die or just be looked after elsewhere. She is a reactor to the independent desires of women. If a Lilith woman is frightened to or reluctant to have children then Lilith will take care of it and from infertility problems to complete barrenness Lilith will provide. So gynecological problems are often blamed on Lilith by some modern Pagans and ancient Hebrews alike.

But as said above she can also play the role of over protective mother. That the spiritual Lilith has offspring we know, albeit demonic ones. Ones that get specific names are beings such as Naamah/The lesser Lilith. Cain in a spiritual sense in so much as he was sired by Lilith and Samael who encouraged Eve to have sex with Adam whilst menstruating, something Judaism and other religions forbid as an unclean act. Azazel in so far as he is the angelic child of Lilith and Samael who becomes the leader of the watchers and is

responsible for the earliest forms of metallurgy and cosmetics. Most of the Nephilim were probably Lilith inspired beings.

Her magical ability to protect her children from harm could, in theory, come from her knowing the name of 'God'. To put this into context she is capable of sharing the mystical and magical knowledge needed to ultimately protect those she cares about from harm. So she is rebelling against both the beliefs and dogma of her origins but also those indoctrination's that ask us to trust in an invisible 'God' to protect us from harm. She is all about taking responsibility for ourselves. She can share with us occult or hidden wisdom that enables us to take care of ourselves. We can use rituals to call on her and ask her to protect us from the harmful effects of her energy but as to literally offering her protection from others she is more likely to imbue us with exactly the right information necessary to do this for ourselves. She is an enabler.

My path has until very recently been purely intuitive. The connection with Lilith was acknowledged, my own inner witch fire was ignited by her and I felt my way from then on. So all my workings and rituals were created from inspired meditations and often included a very basic construct that I found worked sufficiently well at the time. One thing I have done though over the last twelve years or so is build up a very intimate and close relationship with her and a few others she opened me up to such as Lucifer, Azazel, Asmodeus and Samael for the most part. Mine has neither been a celestial or infernal path. It has always rested somewhere between the two. Having a grounding in fae magic and Green Man energy in many of its forms also helped forge a link with her. This seemed to help open a door to her primal realms and some of her many faces. The simplest way I can describe this way of viewing her is to put my own beliefs across.

You can connect with the more complex versions of Lilith and meet each one as an individual. In her purest form Lilith is creative/

Lady Lilith by Dante Gabriel Rossetti

destructive primal energy, the energy that creates worlds. And destroys them. The energy required for life to exist. The Queen of the night and the womb and the Goddess of all life and Gods that followed her. In androgynous form twinned with Samael she becomes the shadow or evil side of life. She was here first. This essentially primitive form of Lilith is chaotic, it gets given form and can be moulded into form but needs very careful handling. This Lilith will wake your own inner plane beast. She will raise your energy but also your libido to insatiable heights and even the slightest hint or sniff of inspiration will be grabbed by her and reflected back at you as a potential reality should you wish it.

Lilith has urged me to look at her roots and the origins of the Abrahamic paths. She has woken me up to the concept of an unseen force of imaginable dimensions but I don't label this as 'God', not in the traditional sense. She inspires us to question our collective spiritual beliefs. And to look at many cultures rather than focusing merely on one.

For those of you who already work with Lilith on a spiritual level this book could be in danger of teaching you to suck eggs. Then again each of us has our own approach so maybe some of what I am about to share could be of use. In many ways I wish I had read up more on her during my early days with her, as it was I took quite a naïve and almost puritanical approach. Many solitary types prefer to feel or find their own way and don't always take the experiences of others into account. This isn't always due to ego or arrogance but can be a need to keep things pure and untainted. I used to live next door to an artist who refused to look at other people's art he felt this was the only way he could ensure this work was authentic. I am sure this rubbed off on me. And perhaps there is a little of this in solitary practitioners. Following your own spiritual nose is exciting, it is personal and although there isn't the safety net of a coven or partner it still has much to commend it. That having been

said Lilith children are frequently attracted to red buttons and I am no exception so many a time she popped up to warn me off a person or situation and I ignored her to my peril. There are many aspects of group ritual and practise that as a solitary you are able to avoid. One frequent complaint many of us encounter in group practise is the rise of the massive ego, the one who always feels the need to Priest or Priestess it up. The one who has to constantly draw attention to themselves through whatever means and comments on all accolades they are given as a reflection of their own self-importance. We all know these types.

Devoting yourself to Lilith is not about glamour or dressing up in robes and waving your arms about it is about getting down and dirty, being prepared to open yourself right up, to let go, but not surrendering to Her, just reaching a point where nothing matters enough to stop your work. Then there are group dynamics and power struggles, back stabbing, and what I term as 'magical paranoia', again all these things can be avoided. In group rituals roles are often given out or awarded and this can also give rise to resentments and upset. So one of the many virtues of solitary practise is that you are the only one performing ritual, you are the only one to answer to. And this in itself can be a massive relief for some people.

Solitary rituals can still take many forms and vary in length and complication. Some people like long drawn out affairs with oodles of paraphernalia and others like to keep things simple. And we all develop methods that work for us. I like simple rituals if possible. Mine are sometimes pre-orchestrated but often take a more organic and intuitive shape. My earliest introduction to magical ritual and invocations was a little Wiccan in origin. The style of ritual I use today is a very simple one and less orchestrated and structured than many available. These might not resonate or seem applicable to you, but it is my feeling that there is no ultimate right or wrong form. I had been introduced to many years ago I found the energy

rose more easily and the effects became more powerful and effective. As Lilith is my main devotion my rituals are very much my own making. They can vary in length from 45mins at the shortest to several hours at the longest. But, occasionally I will remain mindful of the ritual for a few days leading up to the event itself and a few days after so if I take this into account then in some respects they can last days.

Often the intensity of the construct of a pre-prepared ritual can be the most magical part of it. By this I mean that the sheer focus and intent can invoke just as much energy, if not more, as the ritual does. This seems especially true if you are the sort of person who has what is termed as a 'two headed' connection with Lilith as partly an inspiring demon and muse her ability to get into the minds of her children can be subtle and almost unperceived initially and only through greater awareness, meditation and ritual does it become more obvious. So she can start to weave your spells and petitions even before you get as far as actually deliberately invoking her. So the old adage 'be careful what you wish for' is especially relevant here. And it is whilst consciously reading about her that her effects are often strongest. It is easy for many of us to develop a close relationship with Lilith. She is lonely, aloft and adrift, she likes company of those she sees as her kin. So it is also important to be watchful of one of my most common errors that of trying to become possessive over her. This road will lead to many dead ends including the one that finds you sounding like her defence lawyer. Lilith doesn't need defending or reinterpreting, she is what she is, all she has ever been and all she will become. Nor does she require sanitising. If there are aspects of Lilith that you are not at ease with or feel are not her true nature then it is often your own problems with these issues that need addressing rather than anything a particular person or religion has cast against her. As she herself doesn't seem to care why do we? So if you would rather see her as purely a mother Goddess of the night then fine but don't get too

upset if she challenges this and proves you wrong by revealing in her own way, just how much more than this she is. Narrowing her down to only one of her many faces is a mistake I have made as have others.

But even the most solitary of solitaries need some sort of information. And if drawn or called upon to work with Lilith and her family I strongly advise seeking out a more experienced guide or mentor. It helps if you have some sort of basic understanding of how to perform ritual. Rituals can take many forms and involve all manner of objects, times of day or night, moon phases etc. Learning what you can on some of these matters will aid you in choosing auspicious times and also what sort of things you can benefit from using during a ritual. And although there are many forms of protection spells and incantations to ward off Lilith actual callings to her from ancient sources are lacking. So with this in mind most of us who work with her have to be guided by our own knowledge and her inspiration when constructing rituals around her. And although Lilith does have a lighter side to her nature it is not the most of her. She is primeval. And pre-historic in origin. Some might say she was here before any awareness of divinity actually occurred to humankind and therefore she knows us way better than we know ourselves. There is much to Lilith that a single lifetime of devotion will barely scratch the surface of.

Each of us will develop through doing this study and work but it is to the hidden or obscured side of your soul that you turn to whilst in communion with her. How you approach making your connection will vary. When people go to Churches, Mosques, Synagogues and Temples etc. and attend a service they are hoping for a spiritual experience. What they experience will differ greatly even within the same tradition or religion, and this can be unique to each person. Attempts to unify the experience by means of shared ritual will provide commonality and unity but it is also possible for individuals to perceive their own inner plane connection. Shared religious and

spiritual events are the norm across the globe. Solitary religious/ spiritual practises are rarer. For those of you on Lilith's current you have options. If you are able to, then she might provide an open door to a coven or clan that work with her as their main focus. You could also, once experienced enough, begin your own. Or you might be inspired to work with a partner or friend. All these things are possible but one thing I have found with Lilith is that she often inspires solitary practise for a while at least.

This book is designed more for the solitary practitioner. As I have little knowledge and experience of working with others I can only share this perspective. Those who only attend group rituals are often of the opinion that the cohesive energy of the many increases the energy raised, in theory this should be true. Only by trying both can you feel your way towards what works best for you. Equally it is also possible for a solitary ritual to fall flat at the first hurdle. If you prefer to share your spiritual rituals then solitary ones probably won't appeal. For me they are the preferred path. But why? What makes for a solitary 'witch' or 'magician'? Usually we are people who prefer to feel our way intuitively. So sticking to rigid formulas or traditional methods don't always appeal to us. Solitary types are frequently loners, people who like their own company and often prefer it to group activities. We experiment and delve into places that many covens, groups, clans etc. either don't wish to tread or fear to. We don't have to concern ourselves with whether our plans will go down well with others. Considering the needs of the many is not required here. And this alone can appeal to us. Being unilateral in our practise leaves us open to explore any avenue we so wish and often increases our own sense of empowerment. This level of liberation and freedom can be hugely appealing to us. But it comes with great need for responsibility. If it all goes badly wrong, and it can, we only have ourselves to blame and no one to aid us or back us up. So when working at its optimum solitary practise works well for those who are courageous rather than foolhardy, brave rather than

rash and responsible rather than selfish. But many of us will find we fall into either camp at some point or another, it is how we learn. This doesn't mean however that you can't play well with others just that your prefer not to. Some people manage both. This can be useful. As is having at least one experienced mentor able to pick you up and dust you off if you take a tumble.

One of the greatest parts of the Lilith journey is dealing with the preconceived image you already have of her. Overcoming her mythology by immersing yourself in it will be a crucial part of your experience with her, and a hard part. It seems necessary to both embrace and reject it. Almost as if you need to meet all her many faces and let each one weave a web through your life before you can come to terms with this aspect of you reflected in her and vice versa.

You might not be able to deal with this. There could be some of her aspects that you find impossible to reconcile or relate to. As a solitary practitioner this can often throw up the deepest mysteries so running away from her more abhorrent faces is not always a good plan. It is important to retain your own integrity. Lilith can often attempt possession and sometimes gain a partial one but it might be good for you or important to allow this to happen. This isn't about becoming her in a separate sense it is about creating time and space to connect with her and merge with her energy in each of its forms. This level of symbiosis is not always easy to achieve. Some Liliths are more amiable than others. And some take opposing forms depending on which interpretation of her you feel more affinity with. Seeing as we will never know which came first it is entirely up to you which one you feel drawn to work with or call upon first.

It has become apparent to me over the years that a common situation in the occult and magical world is for people to make assumptions and have expectations concerning spiritual entities. Assumptions they often shatter as they reveal to you personally

what they know you actually need at any one time. So I feel it is very important to keep a truly meditative open mind in these situations. And without wishing to sound hysterical or paranoid here opening up through energy raising is potentially dangerous. You will be activating parts of yourself that often lay dormant. You will be vulnerable and exposed until you learn to protect yourself. When someone increases or changes their vibrational level it registers on the astral. This can attract all manner of beings curious about you. Some will be helpful and harmless even beneficent. But some won't. There will be those who like to feed from your energy and some who seek to possess or control it. Even the energy itself can be potentially harmful. If you don't learn to actually use it and direct it in a purposeful way it might turn in on you and cause illness or disease.

I constantly meet very magical people who are wide open. Their energy centres are permanently accessible. These people might well be amazing catalysts or pick up on all sorts of things that intrigue or interest them but they are also laying themselves wide open to attack. And many implode. Many are carrying all sorts of physical, emotional, psychological and spiritual baggage around with them and it is weighing them down. Many begin to get ill or experience pain and often end up with conditions such as chronic fatigue. Although it also seems a part of the path that leads towards healing others to accumulate a few wounds yourself along the way in order to increase sensitivity and empathy. The potential permutations here are endless. And it is tragic, if they had only learned how to open and close to order and protect themselves they would be way healthier and happier and much more efficient magical people.

Once you have decided to take the next step and do a specific ritual to invoke the energy of any particular deity or entity it is not obligatory to follow anyone else's methods. Each coven, clan, group and individual has their own way of doing things. I would not advice deliberately setting out to open up and work magically

with any Lilith or her kin without some basic training or an elder experienced mentor to guide you.

If you are already connected to the Lilith of the Qliphoth and working this side of the Tree of Life then it is most likely the Jewish Lilith or Gamaliel that you are connected with. This form of Qabbala is a popular path among many who bare the mark of Lilith and or Samael. And if so, your workings and rituals may well include aspects of the *Grand Grimoire* or *Verum*. It is perfectly possible to adapt some of the old grimoires and goetia to working with Lilith. And as Queen of Demons most forms of Demonology meet Lilith at some point or another.

Over the years she has lifted me to the greatest of spiritual heights and dropped me in the deepest of holes. She has ripped me apart and turned me inside out and tested me on so many levels I have actually lost count. And maybe it is a mistake to live the legend at times and embroil one's self too deeply in becoming the mythos but it has deepened the connection to the point of being able to tap in and have that two headed link I presume I wanted. Some traditions have much to draw upon for guidance over how to conduct rites and the like, Lilith doesn't. Most of what we have to draw upon when wanting to do any sort of magical work with Lilith stems from the 17th century to modern day. Ancient scripts on Lilith are mostly of the 'warning or beware' variety and more to do with incantations and spells to protect against her than deliberately invoke her. And in some respects this appeals to me. She is not set in any sort of structure or stone temple, hers is that of the wilderness and inner planes.

And so for those of us 'wilder women' and those who are more at peace when alone or breaking a few rules, Lilith is there, always listening, feeling, watching in the shadows.

And always will be.

BIBLIOGRAPHY

Lilith the first Eve – Siegmund Hurwitz; Daimon Verlag;
   ISBN 978-3-85630-732-5.
Interpreting Lilith – Delphine Gloria Jay; American Federation of
   Astrologers Inc.; ISBN 978-0-86690-264-9.
Living Lilith: Four Dimensions of the Cosmic Divine – M. Kelley
   Hunter; The Wessex Astrologer Ltd; ISBN 9781902405346.
The Book of Lilith – Barbara Black Koltuv Ph.D.; Nicholas Hays
Inc.;
   ISBN 089254-014-1.
Lilith Insight – New Light on the Dark Moon; Mae R. Wilson;
   Ludlum, Macoy.
Publishing and Masonic Suply Co. Inc – ISBN 0-86690-347-X.
The Hebrew Goddess – Raphael Patai; Wayne State University
   Press; ISBN 08143-2271-9.
The Cult of the Black Virgin – Ean Begg; Penguin;
   ISBN 0-14-019510-6.
The Mystery and Meaning of the Dead Sea Scrolls –
   Hershell Shanks; Random House; ISBN 0-965-058821.
The Book of Enoch – Translated by R.H.Charles; Society for
   promoting christian Knowledge; ISBN 0-281-05821-0.
The Gilgamesh Epic and Old Testament Parallels – Alexander
   Heidel; University of Chicago Press; ISBN 0-226-32398-6.
Gods, Demons and Symbols of Ancient Mesopotamia – Jeremy
   Black and Anthony Green; British Museum Press;
   ISBN 0-7141-1705-6.
Aramaic Incantation Texts from Nippur – James Alan
Montgomery;
   Cambridge University Press; ISBN 978-1-108-02581-2.

Elizabeth the Queen – Alison Weir; Pimlico; ISBN 0-7126-7312-1.
The King James Bible.
The Talmud.
The Zohar.

Familiar Fingers by Nicholas Messer

www.ingramcontent.com/pod-product-compliance
Lightning Source LLC
Chambersburg PA
CBHW032222080426
42735CB00008B/677